TIME MANAGEMENT
for
SCHOOL
ADMINISTRATORS

by
DR. IVAN FITZWATER

PRO>ACTIVE PUBLICATIONS

Time Management for School Administrators

Published by:

Pro>Active Publications
10 Hale Street
Rockport, Massachusetts 01966

Copyright © 1996 by Pro>Active Publications
Second Printing 1998

Printed in the United States of America

10   9   8   7   6   5   4   3

Main entry under title:

   Time Management for School Administrators

ISBN 1-885432-05-4

Table of Contents

CHAPTER ONE: *Breaking the Stereotype* 1
  A TESTIMONIAL 1
  CRISIS MANAGEMENT 4
  A FINITE RESOURCE 4
  TIME MANAGEMENT = SELF MANAGEMENT 5

CHAPTER TWO: *Identifying the Problems* 6
  THE SCHOOL ADMINISTRATOR'S
  TIME ANALYSIS QUIZ 6
  ADD UP YOUR SCORE 7

CHAPTER THREE: *Getting Organized* 18
  PLANNING AND EXECUTION 19
  THE EIGHTY - TWENTY PRINCIPLE 20
  MOTIVATION THROUGH PLANNING 21
  MODELING 22

CHAPTER FOUR: *Setting Goals* 23
  THE GOAL IN MIND 23
  GOALS MAXIMIZE ACHIEVEMENT 24
  SHARING PERSONAL GOALS 25
  HELPING OTHERS SET GOALS 26
  LUCK ISN'T THE ANSWER 27
  GOALS MUST BE SET CONSTANTLY 27
  A GOAL-SETTING EXERCISE 28

CHAPTER FIVE: *Delegate* 30
  DELEGATION AND PAPERWORK 36

CHAPTER SIX: *Maximize Meetings* 38

CHAPTER SEVEN: *Empower Secretaries* 45
  PUBLIC RELATIONS 46
  OFFICE MANAGER 48
  CONFIDENTIAL COUNSELOR 48
  SPECIFIC GUIDELINES FOR THE RELATIONSHIP 49

CHAPTER EIGHT: *Block Interruptions* 53

CHAPTER NINE: *Master the Telephone* 60
   TELEPHONE USE IN SCHOOLS 60

CHAPTER TEN: *Manage Stress* 69
   SCHOOL ADMINISTRATION IS HIGH STRESS 70
   AN INCREASING PROBLEM 70
   STRESS DEFINED 72
   IMPACT OF STRESS 73
   RESULTS OF EXTENDED EXPOSURE TO STRESS 74
   MANAGING STRESS — AN ACTION PLAN 75

CHAPTER ELEVEN: *Communicate Effectively* 79

CHAPTER TWELVE: *Motivate Staff* 88
   A: ALL PEOPLE BASICALLY WANT TO SUCCEED 92
   B: PEOPLE WORK HARDER AFTER EACH SUCCESS 92
   C: PEOPLE ARE GOAL-SEEKING 92
   D: PEOPLE ENJOY WORK 93
   E: GIVE SUBORDINATES AS MUCH FREEDOM
      AS POSSIBLE 93

CHAPTER THIRTEEN: *Identify Time Wasters* 94

CHAPTER FOURTEEN: *Train the Staff* 103
   A "MINI" TIME MANAGEMENT INSERVICE 104
   A TIME MANAGEMENT TRAINING PROGRAM 105

APPENDIX 106

Author's Introduction

Over the last thirty years I have had the privilege of doing thousands of time management seminars for all kinds of associations, professional organizations and businesses. I have also addressed diverse groups of people where there was no affinity between individuals except their desire to better manage time. These lectures and seminars took me to all fifty states and to at least fifteen foreign countries. I have enjoyed having the opportunity to work with people from all walks of life but, because of my background as a school leader, working with school administrators has been the most rewarding. Thus the opportunity to write a time management book targeted to school executives was a task I assumed with great enthusiasm.

It is true that a generic book on time management is helpful to all people no matter what their line of work. We all have the same amount of time; we each have 86,400 seconds each day to achieve our goals. Thus, in the past, I tried to keep my writings general to address the needs of all people rather than writing for a specific group of profession.

My efforts in this regard were well rewarded as measured by the success of sales of my first two books on this subject. *Finding Time for Success and Happiness*, my first book on time management, was published in 1977 and enjoyed steady sales for ten years. It was supplanted in 1987 by *Time Under Control*, which is still in print and in demand. Both of these books were designed to help any busy person gain control of the time resource, but unlike the present volume neither was designed for a particular job or lifestyle. Each had to be individualized by the reader; the concepts had to be interpreted and customized.

School administration and time management have been parallel passions throughout my career. This book gives me a chance to bring them together, to give special attention to the unique challenges faced by school administrators.

The first chapter looks at the commonly accepted stereotype of how school administrators have to be crisis managers — a view I once held. I relate how a seminar helped me overcome that myth and saved my job and perhaps my life. Then the reader is provided with a diagnostic tool to assist in determining his or her status quo on the use of time.

Subsequent chapters start with the foundations such as planning and goal-setting and progress to narrower and less fundamental topics such as interruptions, the telephone, etc. Every chapter sets a goal and discusses the practices proven most successful in attaining it.

The final chapter and Appendices present a training program designed to help the reader use the knowledge acquired from reading the text to educate others. In the Appendices guidelines are offered, so that readers can create their own mini-seminars for inservice training in time management. Detailed agendas are offered for use as handouts and transparencies in training courses.

In the chapters to follow, I share ideas learned from thousands of school leaders. My hope is that your professional and personal life will be enriched by these ideas as mine has been, that the time of your life will be made more productive and enjoyable by the suggestions put forth.

Ivan W. Fitzwater
San Antonio, Texas
November, 1995

CHAPTER ONE

Breaking the Stereotype

It is possible to be a principal, superintendent or other school administrator and still be calm, in control and happy. The prevailing stereotype is just the opposite, but this view does not have to be accepted as a mandate.

This conviction comes from the experiences of thousands of school administrators who decided to take charge of their lives by employing the tools available through time management. Peoples' lives tend to be self-fulfilling prophecies; the challenge is to construct a prophecy which will bring the desired results — success and happiness. This book describes the procedures which can be used to achieve these goals.

It is not easy to get some school administrators to alter their view of how educational leaders should behave. They have seen men and women in these positions work long hours, harassed by pressures from within and without, as they attempt to manage an impossible workload. A humorist described this situation by telling of the school administrator who died and went to Hades and was there three days before he realized he was not in his office.

Such expectations must change if improvement is to occur. Leaders who accept the status quo as inevitable will continue to suffer unnecessarily. Those who have had difficulty managing time can be assured there is hope. Administrators who have felt spread too thin and believe that the only way to keep up is to put in long hours and take work home will be elated to find this isn't inevitable.

Those who think vacations are just for people in other professions will be pleasantly surprised. It is possible to be firmly in control of your job and still have time for family, recreation and fun. It requires new approaches, the adoption of efficiencies that can cause more to be done with less effort by working smarter, not harder.

A TESTIMONIAL

When I was a workaholic, I did not know I had a problem because I had accepted my lifestyle as normal. My superintendent diagnosed my situation. He realized that my heart was in the right place, that I worked hard and wanted to do a good job. He also realized that I had become a workaholic because I lacked the skills for managing my time. At his urging, I attended a time management seminar and found it to be a life-changing experience.

When I implemented the techniques learned in that workshop, I became much more productive while working fewer hours and having more time for my family. Work became more enjoyable for me and my staff. I attended the seminar reluctantly and literally returned an evangelist for the cause.

1

Colleagues saw the change and were curious to learn what had caused this transformation. When I told them about the seminar and shared with them what I had learned, I found the information was as helpful to them as it had been to me.

My recovery was dramatic but my problem had developed gradually. I was a workaholic when I was a classroom teacher and the disease grew worse as I moved to guidance counselor, junior high-school assistant principal, elementary principal and then high-school principal. As my leadership obligations increased, I tried to extend my work day sufficiently to get everything done. I was not unlike other school leaders whom I observed and so didn't think anything was out of the ordinary. I didn't expect to work a normal work day like most of the other people in my neighborhood. I just thought the pain went with the position. Nothing in my college courses alerted me to this incorrect attitude; indeed, most of what I learned reinforced such thinking.

There are degrees of workaholism and, by the time I spent a couple of years at a high school, the situation was becoming extreme, and I was reaching the point that my health was beginning to suffer. Overwork, lack of exercise and poor eating habits caused me to put on weight. The frantic pace with unproductive results brought on a feeling of frustration. The pressure never eased. Even on holidays or vacation, I always felt I was looking over my shoulder.

In my role as high-school principal, I was reacting to my environment rather than taking control of it. My practice was to arrive at school early in the morning and head for my office hoping to avoid those teachers who came to my office everyday. I didn't realize that by seeing these few each day, I was encouraging behavior which I did not want to see repeated and was ignoring the needs of the vast majority of my employees.

At this school teachers had to be at work by 8 o'clock. Students were admitted at 8:30 and homeroom began at ten minutes before 9:00. If I could engage in activities in my office until homeroom started, there was a possibility that I could avoid these unnecessary and nonproductive conferences with the teachers who came. In an attempt to avoid a few staff members, I was avoiding all of them.

The time management seminar which I attended demonstrated that this approach was wrong. One day our seminar leader had us do an activity which revealed why it was wrong. He asked us to write down the five most important things that we had to do in our job. At the top of my list I had teachers and other employees and below them, students, followed by community relations, physical facilities and finance.

The leader next asked us to take out our calendar and show where we had scheduled these five top priorities. The point was made. The things I listed as my five most important duties were things I had not scheduled. My calendar was full of appointments and other commitments, but in terms of my actual expenditure of time, the top five priorities were missing.

2

It was demonstrated that, if we were to reach maximum effectiveness as leaders, we must synchronize our priorities with time utilization. I saw the logic in this thinking but at first could not figure how to implement the concept, given the realities of everyday life as a principal.

After a few false starts, I finally hit upon a plan that began to revolutionize my effectiveness as a leader. I arrived at school early, just as I had before, but instead of hiding in my office, I walked the halls of the school. The period of time between 8:00 and 8:30 was when the teachers were at work, but the students had not entered the building. I found in that half hour I could make contact with virtually every member of the staff every day and, in doing so, could make a dramatic improvement in the climate of the school.

For example, I would walk into the teachers' lounge and find a group of staff members. When I would say, "Good morning, ladies and gentlemen," they smiled and returned my greeting cheerfully. During the morning walks, I would speak to the teachers who were in their classrooms. They returned my "Good morning!" with great enthusiasm.

I carried with me a list of the teachers who had been absent the day before. When I would see one of them, I would make a special point of inquiring how they felt and remind them how I had missed them the day before. This message of caring seemed extremely important to all of them.

Interruptions to my office dropped to near zero because teachers no longer lined up to see me. I would hear them say to each other, "He will be around in the morning; let's ask him then." My staff counted on me to make contact with them first thing in the morning, and this was a great motivator.

At 8:30 I remained in the hallways when students arrived. To my surprise, many of the students did not even know who I was. I remember the morning that a young student came up to me and said, "Are you a teacher or a person?" I realized then I needed to do more to remain in touch with the student body.

When homeroom began, I returned to my office. Another thing that I had learned was to give my secretary authority to complete any task which arrived in our office if she had the necessary information. This was all my secretary needed to release her energies and use all her intellectual skills. When I arrived, I found that most of the paperwork was completed and ready for my signature. By 10 o'clock I walked out of my office and suddenly realized I had accomplished more by 10 o'clock than I usually accomplished in a whole day. Everybody in the entire enterprise benefitted from my change in behavior.

3

CRISIS MANAGEMENT

Leaders must take control of their lives so they are not at the mercy of the world. Priorities must be set so the needs of the organization occupy their attention rather than the whims of individuals. They must not become reactors where important matters get swamped by trivia, thus making them very busy doing things of little importance. This can cause the expenditure of a lot of energy with little reward, and unplanned reaction leads to frustration.

Instead of being firefighters, leaders must become fire preventers. As tasks of varying importance are experienced, priorities are established so the treadmill with its frenzied activity and state of constant crisis is avoided. They must step off the treadmill, look at what they are doing, make changes which permit them to become more productive. They can debunk the prevailing stereotype and accept the premise that fire prevention techniques such as advanced planning can alleviate management by crisis. The techniques in the chapters to follow for making positive changes are simple, effective and immediately applicable. They require an open mind and a willingness to try. The positive changes that result will increase productivity and foster a calmer environment.

> # TIME MANAGEMENT HELPS SCHOOL ADMINISTRATORS GET OFF THE TREADMILL.
> # THEY GET MORE DONE IN LESS TIME BY DOING THINGS DIFFERENTLY.
> # THE RESULT IS A CALM, ENJOYABLE AND PRODUCTIVE LIFE.

A FINITE RESOURCE

Many school administrators balance a productive professional life along with a satisfying personal life because they have set goals that create balance. They accept the fact that time has to be used for everything in life and not just work. For example, activities that promote good health must be given proper consideration or ultimately lack of vigor or illness causes problems at work.

Lack of attention to family obligations can cause problems that impair effectiveness on the job. Inadequate attention to professional involvement such as attending conventions and other meetings can cause stagnation. School administrators especially must make conscientious allocation of their time because of the diversity of their job, unusual schedules, and the variety of publics they serve.

It is a cliché but true: there is no way to get more time. Everything must be given an amount of time relative to its importance. Work is a vital part of life but only one part of the whole.

TIME MANAGEMENT = SELF MANAGEMENT

Time cannot be borrowed, stored, or recycled; it can only be spent as it is received, twenty-four hours in each day. Thus, time management means self management, managing oneself with respect to a noncontrollable resource.

This realistic assessment, so simple yet profound, causes the emphasis to be correctly placed and enables people to find the secret for taking control of their lives. This recognition of the uniqueness of the time resource helps them avoid pitfalls of incorrect thinking, i.e., "If I get more time," "Time flies," "I'll do it if I get around to it."

School administration has the potential to bring great satisfaction to those who do this important work; it can even be fun. It can also be very unpleasant for administrators who lose control of themselves. In the future, parents, taxpayers and a multitude of groups and organizations will demand attention, while teachers will need more guidance because of the accelerating pace of change in education. These challenges will grow rather than diminish. School leaders, more than most other managers, must understand how to effectively manage time.

CHAPTER TWO
Identifying the Problems

The myth that school administrators must, because of the nature of the job, be hassled and harried has been debunked in the discussion in Chapter 1. The present chapter contains a diagnostic instrument designed to help the reader identify areas that need improvement. Areas of strength will be revealed and reinforced, and weaknesses identified for improvement through the interpretations provided. Each statement should be read and answered according to the way the individual taking the test currently behaves.

When the test is finished, a score will be derived for the reader along with an interpretation of the score. A discussion of the concept embodied in each question will be revealed, and a few time-saving suggestions will be offered as a prelude to more extensive, in-depth coverage of the topics in subsequent chapters.

THE SCHOOL ADMINISTRATOR'S TIME ANALYSIS QUIZ

✐ *Encircle the answer most like you.*

1. My day is often less productive than I had hoped because of unexpected interruptions. .... yes   no

2. My secretary organizes the mail so the most important letters are on the top of the stack and the junk mail is underneath. .... yes   no

3. When I think of a routine telephone call which I need to make, I do it immediately to get it off my mind. .... yes   no

4. My subordinates are encouraged to bring problems to me promptly before they become protracted. .... yes   no

5. I get my office routines and paperwork done before lunch so I can visit with my staff in the afternoon. .... yes   no

6. My subordinates feel they are required to attend too many meetings. .... yes   no

7. I want to be available to my staff so I maintain an open-door policy. .... yes   no

8. Getting something completed, even a small task, is the best way to start the day. .... yes   no

9. When I am late for a meeting or appointment, it is usually because of circumstances beyond my control. ....yes   no

10. Some of my employees are not enthusiastic about their work. ...yes   no

11. I find myself reminding people about deadlines. ....yes   no

12. Skipping lunch is one technique I use to catch up when I get behind in my work. ....yes   no

13. I sometimes put off making decisions until the last possible minute. ....yes   no

14. My desk is a cluttered with paper when I leave at the end of the day. ....yes   no

15. Things are hectic around my home in the morning before I go to work. ....yes   no

16. I occasionally schedule a vacation or holiday, then cancel it because of pressures. ....yes   no

17. It has been over a year since I had a physical examination. ....yes   no

18. Friends and relatives have sent me letters which I have yet to answer. ....yes   no

19. Each time a school administrator is promoted, the amount of paperwork will probably increase for that individual. ....yes   no

20. I would do more research, writing and other creative activities if I had more time. ....yes   no

ADD UP YOUR SCORE

Number marked "Yes" _____

Number marked "No" _____

The purposes of this activity are preview, overview, and diagnosis. To achieve the preview and overview there will be a discussion of the content area highlighted by each statement. The derived score provides the diagnosis as follows.

The answer to every question should be "No" for the reasons that will be given in the discussion as the quiz is reviewed. A lot of "Yes" answers are not uncommon; most school administrators will have ten or more. Every "Yes" can be looked upon as an opportunity to make changes to improve performance in work and provide a more pleasant personal life. In the discussion of each question the comments and illustrations are designed to be of particular assistance to the unique needs of school leaders.

1. *My day is often less productive than I had hoped because of unexpected interruptions.*

A plan must be made so the school leader maintains control, or else other people's priorities flood in and the leader reacts to situations which may or may not be important to the organization as a whole. Leaders must be committed to important tasks, so compelling reasons can be given for being unavailable. This does not mean isolation from subordinates but rather makes the administrator available on a planned basis in the best interest of the total school or school district.

Administrators should start the day by making a list of all the things that must be done that day. Then a check is put beside the most important item on the list, and that job is done first. One task at a time should be done rather than trying to work on several things at once. If anything is left undone at the end of the day, it should be the least important thing and diversions from the list should occur only in genuine emergencies.

It is best to meet with the secretary first thing each morning. In that brief meeting, everything should be given the secretary which is to be done that day. In this way the individual can plan the work and work the plan. No additional task should be given during the day unless it is an emergency.

It is possible for the leader to set a very bad example by interrupting subordinates on a whim and reducing their ability to maintain control. Sensitivity to this must be maintained because it is unlikely that employees will tell their superiors that they feel unduly interrupted by them.

2. *My secretary organizes the mail so the most important letters are on the top of the stack and the junk mail is underneath.*

Junk mail should not be in the stack at all. Handling the mail is a task that should be done primarily by the secretary with the administrator having very little involvement. Training of the secretary will be necessary and guidelines must be established so this key person can make a maximum contribution in this particular area.

For example, when the mail arrives, the secretary throws away all junk mail unopened. This will normally be about one third of the mail. Another third of the mail is routed to other offices for completion and the secretary can do this using the administrator's routing slip. When the two meet each morning to start the day, the secretary will inform the administrator of the mail which came and what was routed to other offices. If there is disagreement about the action which has been taken, it is a relatively minor thing to retrieve what has been sent. Experience reveals that this rarely happens because the secretary can make as good a decision as the administrator.

The remaining mail requires a reply from the office to which it was addressed, but again, the secretary can play a key role. When the letter arrives, the secretary reads it and prepares a reply for the administrator's signature. The secretary is not taking a risk because the administrator will see it before the letter is mailed. If the administrator disagrees with the letter as it is written, a change can be made. But this will rarely happen if proper training has been done.

If the secretary receives a letter and does not feel confident in writing a reply, then at the morning meeting, the leader can tell the secretary what the gist of the reply should be. By the next morning, that letter is completed by the secretary and ready for the administrator's signature.

When this kind of secretarial task is recommended, some feel that the secretary will be overworked. This is really not true because the streamlining eliminates tasks which do not need to be done.

For example, the secretary who has permission to handle mail including writing the letters will not have to take dictation, do transcription, handle junk mail, etc.

The approach also uses the higher-level skills of the secretary and meets this person's need for self-actualization. Some of our best motivational researchers indicate this is a primary need of secretaries, who often have great talent but unchallenging jobs. People are happiest when challenged to use their higher-level skills. The response to this question assumes that a secretary is available to the administrator, which may not always be the case. However, the same concepts can be applied if there are parent volunteers, student helpers or other assistants.

3. *When I think of a routine telephone call I need to make, I do it immediately to get it off my mind.*

Making routine calls can be delegated to the secretary. Each time a routine call needs to be made, it can be noted and instructions can be given at the morning meeting. When calls go from secretary to secretary, there's rarely need for a call back.

When an office is called, it is best to let the secretary know immediately the reason for the call. Often one can get the desired information without having to wait to speak to the administrator. It is also possible to have the secretary get the answer needed and then call it back to the original office. Administrators should have the goal of making only one call on a given matter; this technique accomplishes that because in either case the matter is concluded with no further effort.

When routine telephone calls are delegated, it eliminates the chance of being caught in unnecessary conversation that goes beyond the information actually needed. Most people have had the experience of calling on a routine matter and getting involved in discussions of everything from football games to rumors about fellow employees.

If the leader decides to make routine calls, it is best to make a note of each and do them all at a certain time each day. Making a number of routine calls at one time reduces the length of each individual call by maintaining a wholesome pressure to keep calls brief.

9

4. *My subordinates are encouraged to bring problems to me promptly before they become protracted.*

In some school districts, there is a bottleneck at the top because the system of decision making encourages each problem to flow to the chief executive officer. In the interest of saving time and in making the most of all staff members, the emphasis should be upon making the decisions at the very lowest level in the organization. The only time a problem moves to the next higher level in the hierarchy is when it is an unusual problem, something quite out of the ordinary and certainly not a routine matter.

This means all staff members must be thoroughly trained to do their jobs completely, and it also means that sufficient authority has to be delegated so that leaders at all levels have the power and confidence to act. The organization works best when all administrators have been educated to be skilled problem solvers. Inservice training in problem-solving can repay the organization rapidly and many times over. Schools that employ site-based management must have such training for all personnel.

It is easy to fall victim to "analysis-paralysis," particularly if the problem is controversial or if the proper solution to the problem requires an unpleasant action. This requires discipline, so deadlines are set and decisions are made as soon as all of the data are in. This does not mean that hasty decisions are made or that action is taken before all essential information has been gathered. It does mean that procrastinating in decision making wastes time and usually causes the decision to be less effective.

Being a leader does not mean taking on other people's problems. Instead, assistance is given to subordinates, so they develop the skills necessary for independent action. This can best be done by asking them to define the problem, come up with possible solutions, and look ahead to the consequences that each solution would likely entail.

When a proposed action satisfies the leader, subordinates can put the plan into operation assured of support. When the solution works, they get the credit and grow in the process. Also, they are committed to the solution and will work hard for its success because it is their own rather than one given to them by a superior.

It is also important, when authority is delegated, to have a clear understanding of the limits of administrative power. For example, if site-based teaching teams are used, it is imperative that they know where their authority begins and ends.

5. *I get my office routines and paperwork done before lunch so I can visit with my staff in the afternoon.*

Office routines are low in priority for the effective leader. Thus, they should be done later in the day after more important activities have been undertaken. Employees work best when the leader contacts them first thing in the morning.

They see their administrator smiling, so they know that all is well. Until subordinates get this sort of message from leadership, they may be tentative because of the uncertainty. This leadership technique may seem minor but in reality is not. Generally referred to as a "sense of humor" (a generic term for all positive character traits), the leader who possesses such a sense and makes frequent contact with the staff will greatly stimulate their efforts.

Leadership is, in reality, releasing the energies of other people. The first priority must be to take action to achieve this and leave routines and low priority tasks for later in the day. High on our "To Do" list must be the activities that inspire people and cause them to make their maximum contribution.

6. My subordinates feel that they are required to attend too many meetings.

The quality of meetings held in an organization has a great deal to do with the morale of the employees. For example, several studies reveal that teachers dislike faculty meetings more than any other part of their jobs. It is imperative that as few meetings be held as possible and that the meetings be done effectively, i.e., start on time, don't repeat for latecomers, etc.

Principals should use a consent agenda. Information such as announcements should be sent out in advance because these need not be discussed. The leader starts the meeting by asking the teachers if they have any questions about anything on the consent agenda. If there are no questions, then these items are accepted. Then the presider says something like, "Now let's meet long enough to take up the things we need to discuss and that way we can have fewer meetings and shorter meetings."

When subordinates feel there will be as few meetings as possible and that meetings will be as short as possible, they come to the meetings with enthusiasm because they feel they are being rewarded for their participation.

7. I want to be available to my staff so I maintain an open-door policy.

It is best for administrators to maintain what is called a variable-door policy. This means that the office door is closed a majority of the time. But before this is done, there is an understanding among the people who work together. All acknowledge that, when the door is closed, this is a signal the occupant wishes to avoid distractions. Persons also recognize they can simply knock once and enter if they have something urgent.

Colleagues understand, if the matter is not really urgent, they should jot it down until the next time the door is open. Leaders must also set a good example by doing the same for subordinates.

When the door is open, it is also important that the occupant not face the door. It is better to turn the desk so that a person's side or back is to the door and thus not encourage unnecessary interruptions. When one faces the door and someone passes and looks into the office, the passerby has to speak or risk being perceived as impolite. Such greetings often lead to an unnecessary conversation.

8.   *Getting something completed, even a small task, is the best way to start the day.*

The beginning of the day is the time when people have the most energy and the lowest error rate. This is the time to tackle the most important and the most difficult tasks. If important jobs are put off until later in the day, they will be done when the least energy is available and the error rate is highest.

Many of these concepts are just as important in one's personal life as in his or her professional life. For example, on the weekend, it is advisable to get together with family members on Saturday morning to make a comfortable schedule for the weekend. In this way family activities can be given priority allocation of time.

Some resist this. They don't want to make a schedule on the weekend because they want to be free. If a schedule is not made on the weekend, the most likely thing to be left out is free time. They end up working all weekend without having time for family activities, health needs and recreation, and thus vital areas of life receive insufficient emphasis.

9.   *When I am late for a meeting or appointment, it is usually because of circumstances beyond my control.*

It is generally thought that lateness is caused by emergencies. In fact, this is rarely the case. People are usually late because of bad habits. Some people are always late, while others are always on time. It is unreasonable to believe that one person would have emergencies all the time, and another would have none.

It is easy to predict who will be late for a meeting because it's usually the ones who live the closest. If someone has to go a great distance to a meeting, they plan ahead and arrive early. If the meeting is nearby, it is easy to take for granted that they will be on time and then end up being late.

Often it is the leader who actually causes people to be late. For example, if meetings don't always start on time and people come on time only to be punished for their promptness, then they are unlikely to come on time in the future. Fortunately, the staff will also respond to positive cues. If meetings consistently start on time and thus, those who are prompt are rewarded for their positive behavior, tardiness is likely to disappear.

10. *Some of my employees are not enthusiastic about their work.*

A primary obligation of leaders is to make sure that subordinates are motivated to give their best to the organization. It is not sufficient to blame lack of productivity on uninspired employees. There are techniques to reach them. A variety of approaches must be used until even the most reluctant staff member is invigorated.

This means that administrators must get out of their offices and show by their presence that they are truly interested in what staff members are doing. One proven way is to "catch them doing right" and praise all staffers for their good work. If employees work in a situation where they know their good efforts will be noticed and rewarded, they are more likely to work hard. One researcher observed that a compliment from a superior is equal to twenty from colleagues.

A teacher told about the day her principal came by her classroom and stayed just a few minutes. At the end of the day she found a note in her mailbox commenting on several positive things the principal observed. This had a tremendous positive impact on her. She said she called her parents that night and read them the note. The next day she came to work with renewed vigor because her principal had complimented her work. "This act by my superior caused me to work with great enthusiasm for a long time afterward," she said.

11. *I find myself reminding people of deadlines.*

The best way to get people to meet deadlines is to set them cooperatively with the person who is going to perform the work and then never overlook a deadline. When deadlines arrive, the work should be called for without exception. Once people understand that deadlines are never overlooked, they will respond to that expectation, just as they will be careless if deadlines are not enforced.

An effective technique used by many leaders is to employ a tickler file to manage deadlines. A box of index cards with thirty-one dividers for the days of the month and twelve more dividers for the next twelve months can be used. When a task is given to someone, the person receiving the task is involved as much as possible in the structuring of the assignment. They are encouraged to react to the proposed deadline and make suggestions and ask questions. The leader does not tell them how to do the job but instead they agree on what is to be accomplished; the task is assigned in *outcome* terms. This gives maximum ownership to the person doing the work, which is important for motivation.

After agreement is reached between the two regarding what is to be accomplished, a blank card is taken from the box and the finished product (including the deadline) is described. The card with the agreement is placed in the box behind the date when it is due. The secretary checks the tickler file first thing in the morning. When any task is due but not submitted, a call goes out immediately.

When a tickler file is used consistently, the problem of missed deadlines is diminished or eliminated because everyone knows deadlines will not be overlooked. For example, the college professor who does not accept late assignments except in life or death emergencies will experience little wasted time compared to those who do not have such standards. The professor who permits "incompletes" will spend hours on unnecessary follow-up and conflict.

12. *Skipping lunch is one technique I use to catch up when I get behind in my work.*

Productivity is more likely to stay high when workers reward themselves for good work. If rewards are not received, the intensity of effort is lessened and productivity goes down. For example, when people know that if they complete a certain amount of work they can have a pleasant lunch hour, then they are more likely to work in such a way that the reward is achieved. Conversely, if they work in the morning with a mind set that they might have to work through lunch, their productivity will probably go down, and that prophecy will be fulfilled.

If they leave home in the morning and tell their families they will be home at 5:30, work intensity increases. The thought of getting home incites them and causes them to work hard to achieve the goal.

13. *I sometimes put off making decisions until the last possible minute.*

Management by deadline can result in shoddy work being done and many tasks having to be done over. It saves time and a great deal of frustration when things are done right the first time. This requires planning and proper <u>anticipation of deadlines</u> to avoid doing work at the last minute and in a rush.

When projects are assigned to students, it is important to give them enough advance notice and interim checkpoints along the time-line so that they can do an excellent job. Otherwise, some students will put the assignment off until the last week before the project is due. This results in poor quality work far below what they would be capable of achieving if they started firmly, progressed steadily and avoided the last-minute rush.

Fortunately, most students avoid management by deadline by anticipating how much time will be required to do an excellent job and then setting short-term goals within the overall project. They decide how much work will have to be done each week to have the term paper finished ahead of the deadline. This also permits them to enhance their work by building in time for review and revision

14. *My desk is cluttered with papers when I leave at the end of the day.*

A cluttered desk is a symptom of disorganization and a thief of time. Some people deny the truth of this statement by claiming they know where everything is on the desk. What really happens is that they are constantly being interrupted by the papers on the desk.

This premise can be tested by simply putting a dot on a paper each time it is picked up and then put back down without being completed. The papers catch "chickenpox" as they are handled over and over again.

A better way is to start each day with an absolutely clean desk and end each day with a clean desk. Only one task at a time should be on the desk and that is the task which is currently being worked on. There should be no telephone, pen set, pictures or other items on the desk. These should be placed on a table beside or behind the desk.

The in-basket should be monitored by the secretary and with strict rules for what is placed therein. Whoever puts papers into the in-basket is the person who sets priorities for the office. Incidentally, the in-basket can be a good standby task to do if someone does not show up for an appointment as planned.

15. *Things are hectic around my home in the morning before I go to work.*

Steps must be taken to prevent a hectic beginning of the day because what happens between the time a person rises and goes to work can set the tone for the day. This means that leaders must go to bed early enough to get a good night's sleep so that they will be rested and ready to awaken early in the morning.

Then they should rise early enough to have a leisurely beginning for the day. An unhurried morning should include adequate time for bathroom needs, a chance to read the paper or possibly meditate, and time for an unhurried breakfast. They should leave for work with time to spare, so they do not have to rush. This relaxed beginning to the day will pay dividends as the leader arrives at work smiling and setting a good example for the entire staff.

16. *I occasionally schedule a vacation or holiday then cancel it because of pressures.*

If a high level of performance is to be maintained by school administrators, it is imperative that they have adequate rest and relaxation. Vacations and holidays should not be looked upon as luxuries which can only be afforded by other professions but rather as necessities to maintain peak performance. If planning is done and subordinates are properly trained, canceling vacations will occur only on the rarest of occasions.

One must not feel guilty about taking off time that has been earned, nor should anyone feel indispensable. Good leadership assures there are people who are trained to step in and do the job well. It is probably wise for leaders to be away occasionally to give subordinates a chance to display their competence.

There are school administrators who go on vacation and come back to a desk piled high with all the papers that came in during the period. A better way is to have the person who is filling in make every decision and complete every job while superiors are away. Then administrators return to a clean desk and feel they have indeed had a vacation.

17. *It has been over a year since I had a physical examination.*

The medical profession reports that if all people were conscientious with their health (including an annual physical exam every year after age forty and every two years prior to age forty), the average lifespan would be extended significantly because diseases would be discovered when they give early warning signs. Estimates indicate that five to seven years could be added to the average lifespan if all professionals were conscientious with their health.

When people are asked why they have not gotten a physical exam, they often say they don't have enough time. This is probably untrue because it does not take that long for a good examination. In many cases people do not get sufficient health care because they don't want to hear the physician say, "Slow down, stop smoking, lose weight," etc., the very things they should hear and heed.

18. *Friends and relatives have sent me letters I have yet to answer.*

Such procrastination can be brought on by several causes. Some jobs are not tackled because they are so large they intimidate and others because they are so small they seem unimportant. Failure to write letters probably is due to the latter.

To overcome procrastination the big job should be broken down into a series of little jobs, and then the little jobs can be scheduled. Putting small tasks on the daily list of things to be done can upgrade them sufficiently so that they warrant doing. Making a firm decision as to whether or not a particular task needs to be done can relieve the nagging feeling brought on by uncertainty.

Additionally, writing letters to friends and relatives can be a task set aside for bonanzas of time — time which comes unexpectedly. For example, when a person goes someplace and has to wait, rather than wasting that time, he can take out stationery from his briefcase and write letters, a task that often nags but brings pleasure when completed.

19. *Each time a school administrator is promoted the amount of paperwork will probably increase for that individual.*

Unfortunately, this statement is true for most school administrators, but it doesn't have to be. Paperwork is a low-level activity with little payoff for the leader compared to other activities. Leaders must not be trapped with paperwork when they could be doing something important such as supporting the staff with their presence.

It is imperative that people at each level be required to complete paperwork so it need only be reviewed and approved at the next higher level. Anything that does not need approval at a higher level should not be sent at all.

If people are given sufficient authority to complete their work without involving superiors, much unnecessary duplication can be avoided. If employees are consistently required to complete tasks in a high-quality fashion, time can be saved by reducing turn-downs and resubmissions. The challenge is to discipline everyone so that incomplete or poorly done work will not be offered or accepted, thus saving time and tension for everyone.

20. *I would do more research, writing and other creative activities if I had more time.*

This is obviously a "cop-out" statement because there is no way to get more time. It is one of those meaningless statements which can be used to excuse inefficiency. It is really a question of <u>priorities</u>. Whatever a person is doing is obviously more important than anything else at that time. One must be disciplined to work according to the priorities that pay the greatest dividends in terms of personal goals and the mission of the organization.

The foregoing quiz has provided an overview and introduction to many of the concept areas in the body of knowledge normally termed *time management*. It has also provided the reader information relative to an individual's areas of strengths and weaknesses. This latter effort could be disheartening to a person who discovers vast areas that need improvement.

Such a person should find comfort in the fact that most executives, especially school executives, share this feeling and all are capable of making constructive changes. The chapters to follow contain ideas that have proven effective in practice for thousands of school leaders. There is reason for great optimism for those who go forward with an open mind.

CHAPTER THREE
Getting Organized

In real estate it is said that only three things are important in determining the price of a property: location, location, location. School executives might well borrow from this concept and change it to describe how time must be managed: planning, planning, planning. Failure to organize causes expansion of the time required to do a task, induces uncertainty through lack of purpose and permits a crisis atmosphere to prevail. The specific steps presented in this chapter can be implemented as an antidote for lack of planning and thus save time.

The principal of an elementary school told this story. She said that intellectually she understood the value of planning but had not really incorporated this knowledge into her work. Then one day things were particularly hectic; work was piling up and she was not getting much done because of the telephone and other interruptions.

Finally, because of the chaos, she called, "Time out!" She told her secretary to hold the calls, and she closed the door to give herself a chance to collect her thoughts. She took the various tasks on her desk and organized them one by one in priority order. Then she tackled them one at a time until she got caught up and once again felt in control.

When she experienced the good feeling of being on top of things, she decided she wanted to stay in control. "I suddenly realized I could maintain that feeling if I made being in control my priority and then did what was necessary to make it happen. I also realized that I had been making myself vulnerable to low-priority use of my time by failing to schedule my work. Now I plan my days and I rarely go home in the afternoon with that feeling of having worked hard but of having accomplished little. I plan to continue working this way because I get more done and enjoy work more."

Some people become defensive when planning is discussed, much in the same way they do when a clean desk is recommended. In a workshop one day, the participants were debating the benefits of planning. An obviously agitated principal in the audience stood up to take exception to what was being said. He felt his colleagues were greatly exaggerating the importance of getting organized. The workshop leader attempted to sway him by having him reflect upon his own experience.

He was asked how long he would be away from his office attending the workshop, and he replied three days. He was then asked to describe the last day he spent in his office before he came to the program. His response made a great case for planning.

He said that, since he was going to be away for three days, he went to work early. He made a list of what he wanted to do, so he would not forget anything. He gave his secretary authority to screen calls and visitors and let her handle the mail.

He was then asked how his accomplishments on that day compared to other days in the office. He replied that he got a great deal more done that day and then he added, "I guess I could live that way everyday if I wanted to, couldn't I?" He had convinced himself and made the point of the value of getting organized.

Because of the complexity of school management some administrators report that productivity doubles when they start making a list each morning and then work on one thing at a time in priority fashion. Some find they do an even better job if they make their list the day before. The list is made the afternoon before and is ready for the start of the next day. Either approach will make a great improvement.

It is hard to explain why the simple and effective techniques of planning are so rarely utilized by intelligent people who would benefit greatly from even a modest effort. Indeed, it seems more often that little tasks are more readily planned than larger, more important tasks. For example, when someone prepares to take a trip to a distant city, the person will automatically get a road map and make a plan. They are not as likely to have a plan for their careers or their personal lives. A "road map" can be very beneficial in helping careers accelerate and personal dreams be realized. The following saying is valid here: "It is all right to plan and fail but not to fail to plan."

PLANNING AND EXECUTION

The time required to complete a task is greatly reduced when planning comes first. The desired outcome is pictured, and sequential steps leading to that outcome are developed. The interim steps are then performed in logical order to prevent unnecessary mistakes and wanderings. One minute devoted to such planning can save twenty minutes of meandering activity.

One can imagine what it would be like to try to build a house without a blueprint. The architect begins with the end product in mind and devises a plan with the steps in sequential order leading from the foundation to the roof. Without the blueprint one portion of the house might be constructed and then torn down to build some other part of the structure. The plan insures that it is built right the first time so it is not necessary to rebuild.

The three steps known as the "Cycle of Planning" are valuable tools for leaders. Each time the three steps—**plan, act, evaluate**— are used, a higher level of accomplishment is reached. A job is planned and executed. Then the results are evaluated, and a decision made as to how it might be done better next time. This cycle provides constant growth as planning becomes a habit.

The sponsor of senior class activities in a large high school was known for the beauty and precision of the graduation exercises. When asked how she and her assistants reached such a high level of performance, she gave credit to a process that was really the "Cycle of Planning" in action.

"I have been in charge of graduation for many years," she said. "In the beginning, things went wrong, and the ceremony lacked excitement. But each year, the students and the other teachers on my committee planned together to try to make this activity as beautiful and meaningful as possible and always better than the previous year."

"After graduation is over we sit down together to evaluate how well we met our expectations. We are never satisfied, even though we improve compared to the prior year. Then we identify the things we want to change and thus, even though we never reach perfection, we are constantly growing. When I think back on those early years I can see tremendous improvement."

THE EIGHTY - TWENTY PRINCIPLE

The eighty-twenty principle comes into play in almost every human endeavor, including the way time is utilized. Unless careful planning is done, eighty percent of the time resource will be spent giving <u>trivial</u> attention to work. This lack of intensity means that an eighty percent expenditure of time will produce only a twenty percent show of results.

The remaining eighty percent of work must be completed in the remaining twenty percent of time. This leads to a very predictable last minute rush, an enhanced error rate and unhealthy emotional stress. Lull periods followed by frenzied periods produce much of the crisis seen in the workplace today.

Planning is the key to overcoming the eighty-twenty principle. The day starts firmly according to a conscious plan. The best possible use is made of the precious first hours of the day when energy levels are highest and error rate the lowest. The natural temptation at the beginning of the day is to procrastinate, saying, "I've got all day; there is no rush."

An athletic director told of a school district in Texas that had two different high schools win the state football championship in different years, a rare occurrence. He told how different the personalities of the two head coaches were: one was a high-energy, "hyper" person and the other was quiet and retiring. One sought the spotlight, while the other was content to stay in the background. What they had in common was success in winning year after year including a state championship, something only one percent of coaches will ever achieve.

"I discovered the key to their success," he said. "These two very different individuals did have something else in common besides winning. They both held shorter practice periods than most coaches! The practices were shorter because they were thoroughly planned in advance to make vital use of every minute.

"Both coaches posted a schedule in advance so the players knew exactly what they were to do. When they arrived at practice they were given a certain number of minutes to warm up and do wind sprints. After this they had a predetermined amount of time to work on blocking, etc."

20

"These two coaches held brief, highly structured practices," observed the athletic director. "Planning made the work effective in an economy of time, so long sessions weren't necessary."

MOTIVATION THROUGH PLANNING

A superintendent reported that, when he left the building, less work seemed to be accomplished by his staff. He pondered why this might occur. Upon reflection he theorized that it was probably one of two things: either his employees did not clearly understand what they were supposed to do or they did not feel that they had a part in deciding what was to be done. He concluded that when dealing with professionals such as educators, it was the latter.

People become committed when they are involved, so it is incumbent upon leaders to make sure that all of employees have a chance to make suggestions, ask questions and participate in setting job targets. This can be done in formal meetings or in informal rap sessions. Such participation brings enthusiasm, which causes people to work hard whether or not leadership is present. The time spent in getting people involved in organizational planning is recouped many times over because of the high level of motivation which results from the feeling of "teamness."

The chairman of a department in a middle school reported that he had great difficulty in getting much enthusiasm from his staff.

PLAN FOR SUCCESS

1. DECIDE WHAT IS TO BE ACCOMPLISHED IN OUTCOME TERMS.

2. SELECT A LOGICAL SEQUENCE OF STEPS.

3. SET A REASONABLE TIME LIMIT FOR COMPLETION OF EACH STEP.

4. STAY MOTIVATED AND DISCIPLINED.

5. ENJOY THE INCREASED PRODUCTIVITY, AND FEELING OF CONTROL.

The teachers worked hard, but were not using innovative techniques that would have given zest to their teaching. Little excitement emanated from the classrooms as the teachers plodded on with dull instruction. The chairman brought in new ideas, but these were ignored at first and attacked where he persevered. "The teachers were in a comfortable rut and I couldn't get them out," he said.

"Then a book I read gave me a clue. It suggested that people only implement ideas to which they help give birth. I had been offering them a finished product instead of letting them help with the planning.

"Based upon this knowledge I changed my techniques and approached them with a challenge to make changes which they thought advisable. I let them know that I expected action but I gave them a lot of latitude and I didn't intimidate them with my own feelings. The idea was that they were being given a chance to review their situation and to justify current practices or propose changes.

"To my great and pleasant surprise these formerly reluctant teachers took hold of the situation. Rather than spend their energies ignoring or attacking my plan, they embraced the opportunity to make changes with which they were comfortable. They were good changes. I won't forget that getting people beyond 'ignoring' and 'attacking' requires involving staff members in planning from the beginning so they will be motivated and reach the 'embrace stage.' "

MODELING

Leaders have to be the most optimistic of all employees in the organization. They have to be the keepers of the dream, because if they cannot see hope in a given situation, how can others? The level of enthusiasm in an organization cannot rise above the level of enthusiasm of leadership. Those who lead set the tone reflected by the entire staff.

The level of optimism is not the only attitude of leaders that pervades the organization; behaviors are also imitated. For example, the amount of planning done reflects the emphasis on planning by the superintendent, principal or other school administrator. This means it is imperative that administrators model good planning skills, so that subordinates will do the same. Good planning skills pay dividends for leaders, but, even more importantly, staff members copy this productive behavior.

CHAPTER FOUR

Setting Goals

The story is told of two men who approached a large field covered with new snow. The roads had been obscured, and there was no way to find a direct path across to the distant woods except by one's inherent sense of direction. The two of them made it a contest to see which could walk the straightest path across the unmarked field. As the first man veered first to one side and then the other while crossing the field, he left a very crooked line of footprints. The second walked a line straight as an arrow without any hesitation. His secret: he had fixed his gaze on a tall tree on the other side of the field and kept looking at it while he walked. This kept him from wandering and helped him reach his goal successfully without wasted steps.

This story has a lesson for those who set about improving their lives by wise use of time. A goal must be established for the future and movement made toward it without wasting energy wandering in other directions. Checkpoints must be built in along the way to the goal to ensure maintenance of a realistic schedule. This chapter provides information about effective ways to benefit from setting goals.

THE GOAL IN MIND

Goal setters **begin with the end in mind**. A target such as a desired outcome is described in detail so that there is no confusion about what is to be achieved. The goal is kept in sharp focus, thus permitting maximum release of energies toward a specific objective.

Psychologists say that human beings are by nature goal-seeking. In fact, people can become unhappy and restless when they are without goals to give them a sense of purpose and of being needed. This is a real problem for many older people who retire from work and do not have activities to give meaning and purpose to their lives. It is also true of the assembly-line worker who becomes bored or unhappy doing a routine, unchallenging task. No amount of money seems to compensate for the absence of an inspiring goal, which, while being pursued, gives intent to life and a sense of self worth. This basic human instinct can be capitalized upon to increase productivity and simultaneously enhance personal morale.

Most people have generalized goals. Most want such things as a secure retirement, family and personal happiness, and advancement at work. However, these are not specific enough to have an impact on a daily basis. For example, someone wants to accumulate a certain amount of money by age sixty-five. But without a clearly defined goal, a specific amount of money in mind, the person does not know how much will need to be saved each year or month.

Others want good health at retirement but realize they have not had a physical exam in years. They could have early stages of a disease, which, if left untreated, will make age sixty-five an unreachable goal. Some people talk about old age over a high-calorie lunch and punctuate the conversation with cigarette smoking. Their plans will likely be unfulfilled dreams, because the goals do not have power enough to alter their behavior.

> # LEADERS CAN MAXIMIZE THE CONTRIBUTIONS OF SUBORDINATES BY HELPING THEM SET GOALS THAT REQUIRE THE HIGHEST USE OF THEIR TALENTS AND ABILITIES.

GOALS MAXIMIZE ACHIEVEMENT

A woman had become superintendent of a school district before the age of thirty-five. Someone complimented her and suggested it was quite unusual for someone to reach such a position at her age. Her reply underscored the power of goals to increase a person's achievement. She said, "When I completed graduate school, I set a goal to be a superintendent by the time I was forty years old. I always tried to do a good job in the position that I held but I was also preparing myself for the next step. I had my goal constantly in mind; a sharp picture of where I wanted to go. This helped me make correct decisions and thus accelerate my career beyond even my own dreams."

It is true in all walks of life that those who set goals accomplish more than those who do not. This is most readily apparent in sales-oriented professions where great emphasis is put on competition between salespersons. Those who receive the top awards for super sales achievement, when asked how they did so much more than others in their field, inevitably answer, "I set high goals and I did what was necessary to make them happen."

A very interesting phenomenon is that it appears virtually impossible to set goals too high. In fact, the higher they are set, the more likely they are to be achieved. Psychologists tell us that people rarely use more than about ten to fifteen percent of their abilities. Setting very high goals can cause average people to become superstars by increasing the percentage of ability used to attain the goals.

24

A principal tells the story of how he was designated to represent the educational community in the city where he lived by serving on the board of the community chest (now known as the United Way). The practice had been for board members to get together at the beginning of each year, divide up the territory and then set out to raise money for this important charity. They believed they were doing a good job because the amount of money raised compared favorably with other cities of the same size.

Then a change occurred in the way the charity drive was conducted. They employed a full-time executive director to coordinate their efforts.

The executive director revolutionized the way the fund drive was handled. The first thing he did was to suggest a goal nearly ten times as great as any amount of money they had ever raised. The citizens were stunned by the size of the job before them but were assured they could carry out this great achievement if they tried hard enough.

They amazed themselves by not only reaching but exceeding the very high goal. "What the director did was to motivate us into giving a greater effort than we had ever given before," the principal said. "When we had worked without a specific goal, we did just enough to appease our consciences. With a high, even scary, goal before us, this was no longer possible; we could no longer be satisfied with minimal achievement. It was amazing the difference a goal made."

SHARING PERSONAL GOALS

If goals are set and then not shared with anyone else, there is a great temptation to abandon those goals when the going gets tough. It is usually more productive to develop our goals and then share them in a proper way with appropriate people. The two key words are *Proper* and *Appropriate*.

Proper means that goals are shared in a way that does not involve hubris or being braggadocios. It is also important that goals not become a threat to other people's opportunities to progress. If a teacher says to the principal, "I'm interested in learning everything I can about the operation of the organization and I will be willing to take on extra responsibility in order to give me an opportunity to learn," this is a wholesome way of saying, "I want to get ahead." Of course, the person must be sincere and willing to follow through rather than give lip service only.

Another proper way of announcing goals is during the annual evaluation conference. This is the time when a person can call attention to accomplishments by saying things like, "These are the things that I'm most pleased with and this is what I hope to accomplish during the next year." At evaluation time, people are expected to document and announce their achievements.

Sharing goals with appropriate people could also mean discussing them with a mentor who might also be a superior. Obviously, goals can be discussed with family and with a few trusted friends. Beyond this, discussing our goals with others might not be helpful and could even be counterproductive.

HELPING OTHERS SET GOALS

Leaders should not be judged by what they do with their own two hands but by the productivity of those who work for them. This oft-repeated axiom is certainly true of educational leaders whose reputations rest upon the effectiveness of a total and often diverse staff. One way to increase staff members' contributions is by helping them set individual goals and thus open new vistas personally.

Graduate students are often surprised when they come in to talk with their advisers about educational programs and jobs they will hold in the future. Most have elevated their thinking to a master's degree and an assistant principalship. When the adviser starts talking about the doctorate they could earn and how they could prepare themselves for a principalship or a superintendency, they are often surprised. Many have not pictured these positions as possibilities and grasp only for the first time that these are realistic aspirations.

Leaders have tremendous opportunities to help others develop to the maximum by pointing out talents and abilities which the others may not be aware. They can also help them aspire to much higher achievements than they would have done on their own. They can show confidence in them and thereby cause them to have more confidence in themselves. They can help them understand that ordinary people do extraordinary things by reaching high and working hard.

The principal of an elementary school was discussing with his staff how students could be encouraged to read more books. It was determined that students read an average of ten books each year and the staff agreed this number was far too low.

An idea was proposed to dramatically increase reading. A goal was set to have an average of twenty books read by each student by the end of the semester, which was twelve weeks hence. If attained this would mean a tremendous increase. As an incentive, the principal promised to spend an entire day on the roof of the school if the goal was achieved. The average number of books read was twenty-two!

LUCK ISN'T THE ANSWER

Some people achieve much more than others and this is often attributed to luck. But as someone observed, "When preparation meets opportunity, this is what the world calls luck." Achievers possess an attitude that helps them get ahead; they have a positive outlook on life and they believe they can succeed. Thus they set high goals. It is convenient for those who do not make high achievements to rationalize their lack of success by blaming bad luck.

One of the very best motivational speakers in America has a considerable speech handicap. He quickly puts his audience at ease by making some tasteful jokes pointed at himself. He lets everyone know that the speech impediment is not bothering him and that it will not be permitted to stand in the way of everyone having a good time. He soon has everybody laughing with him and, by the time he starts to make serious points, the audience is scarcely aware of the speech problem.

He had been a quarterback on his college team and his speech impediment was so bad that other players had to call the plays in the huddle. (This was given as one example of how he had found ways to succeed in spite of his problem.) After college he became a successful manager by continuing to find creative ways around his handicap but it bothered him that he could not overcome this nagging obstacle.

One day he decided to confront the problem directly. He set as his goal to become a professional public speaker, to excel in the very area of his weakness. He told about the struggle that ensued, the setbacks, the disappointments, how he doubted at times his goal could ever be reached. But he persevered and in doing so, found ways to turn the handicap into an advantage, which captured the complete attention of audiences. His speech impediment became his "hook" and it was very effective. Everyone came away inspired by the thrilling story of how this man turned a deficit into an advantage which lifted him above his competition. Other speakers without handicaps work for half the honorarium of this man who stutters.

GOALS MUST BE SET CONSTANTLY

When goals are reached, there is generally a period of euphoria, but this is short-lived. If new goals are not immediately established, listlessness, even depression can occur; no accomplishment will bring sustained happiness beyond a brief period. Goal-setting, in all phases of life, must be done continuously to maximize achievements by maintaining focus and high motivation.

A GOAL-SETTING EXERCISE

This exercise is provided so the reader can determine whether time is being spent on the things in life that are most important as determined by life goals. To do this exercise only a piece of paper and a pencil will be needed. The instructions are as follows:

Take three minutes to do each of the following things:

1. **Make a list of your lifetime goals**. These goals can be career, family, religious, civic, or anything else. It is imperative that five to ten of the most important ones be selected.

2. Take another three minutes and **write down your goals for the coming year**, a few of the most important ones.

3. At this point you are asked to do something that sounds ridiculous, but please take it seriously because it has an important purpose. Pretend you just learned that you have only one month to live, but the doctor says you are going to have reasonably good health right up to the last day. **If you knew you had exactly one month to live, what would be the goals you would want to accomplish during that month?** Write them down in three minutes.

4. This is the final step in the exercise and the real test of whether or not your time is being spent on your true goals. **Take three minutes and write down everything you have done in the last two weeks toward accomplishing any of the goals that you have listed above.**

Were you pleased when you wrote down the things you have done in the last two weeks toward your goals? Were there large gaps? Did you find that some of the very important things of your life had not been given any of your time in the last two weeks?

Many people find they have nothing to write down in terms of what they have done recently toward reaching their goals even in areas which they consider the most important aspects of their lives. If this happened in your case, you will certainly want to restructure how you spend your time in the future. For example, if you had your family at the top of your list, today you can take your calendar and decide how many nights each week you want to stay home so that you will know how many nights you have to give to other good and worthy causes after the number one priority is satisfied.

Some people find their lifetime goals are not really goals at all. They find that they have written down pleasantries such as, "I want to be a good father," or mother or spouse. These are generalized statements and not really goals; goals have to be specific and measurable. Goal statements are written thus, "I want to spend three nights each week with the children," or "with my spouse." These become goals because they can be measured and a determination can be made about progress or lack thereof.

28

Most people list their really important goals when they think they have just one month to live. They become very specific and write things like,"Take the family trip we've been putting off," or "Call someone up and tell them how much we appreciate them," or "Get right with God." In truth, life would probably be more productive and satisfying if everyone lived as if they had just one more month of life. Important things would not be deferred nor would any one obligation such as work get more time than deserved.

CHAPTER FIVE

Delegate

School administrators report that improvement of delegation techniques often provides them the greatest help in getting control of their jobs. The National Academy for School Executives has made this topic the centerpiece of its Executive Renewal Seminar for the last seventeen years. The reason is simple; participant evaluations reveal year after year that sharpening delegation skills is the most enlightening of all the topics. These same participants report that, six months after the seminar, they have gained an average of one hour per day because of improved delegating.

A teacher told how she revolutionized her classroom after attending a time management inservice. She admitted to being skeptical before the workshop, but to her surprise, the information she gained was beneficial to her as a classroom teacher. And the discussion of delegation was the most helpful of all. Before the workshop she said she was unhappy because she was working hard, but her students were not.

"Students learn best when they are active," she said, "But I was permitting them to be passive. I found that I needed leadership skills because I was having to 'manage' one hundred twenty subordinates each day."

She was teaching the students to write paragraphs but because she had five classes, she could only have them write a paragraph about once each week; then they would have to wait while she graded the papers. By the time she gave the essays back, the students had forgotten what they had written. Most of her efforts were wasted because the students simply looked at the grade and then put the papers in their desks without reading the critiques. She devoted virtually all of her available time, including evenings, to grading papers but still could not get them back to her students in a timely fashion.

She knew that students learn to write best by writing constantly. "They do not learn vicariously by watching someone else write or by being told how to write. If students are going to really learn, they must practice a lot," she said, "but I wasn't able to do that with the procedures I was using."

"After the time management training, I really changed things, she said. "I started having my classes write a paragraph every other day. The second day we graded the papers in class with the students doing most of the work. I divided the class up into Specialty Groups. One was the punctuation specialty group and another was the capitalization group, theme sentence group, etc. I divided up the papers among the groups and then periodically rotated the groups based upon their assignments. Incidentally, problems with discipline virtually disappeared because now the students were busy doing something all of the time."

30

She said the results were amazing; she had never seen students learn punctuation as well as they did when they were responsible for the grading. "They saw how the other students wrote, so their realm of learning was increased. If they had questions, I was right in the room to answer them," she said, "but they rarely ever did."

"The students were now writing the amount I knew was necessary for maximum learning, discipline ceased to be a problem and the students were happy. I achieved this by delegating authority to my students and requiring them do everything of which they were capable. There was also a wonderful benefit for me, personally. I now had no papers to take home for grading and so I could spend evenings with my family!"

This is an excellent example of what occurs when leaders make it a goal to delegate maximum authority. The efficiencies that result streamline the operation, causing more work to be done at the very lowest level possible. In the example just given, the students contributed more and consequently learned more when the teacher involved them in all facets of the learning process.

A high-school principal reported excellent results after he learned the possibilities afforded by enhanced delegation. He had four assistant principals, and it had been his practice to have each of them do one fourth of the discipline for the school. After each assistant principal worked with a student, a sheet of paper was filled out detailing the actions taken. Each Friday the assistant principals turned the sheets into the principal, who spent Friday afternoon reviewing these reports. He did not really do anything with them but felt it was necessary for him to review them, so that he was properly monitoring discipline in the school.

His new awareness of the value of delegation caused him to change this system. He informed the assistant principals that the reports would no longer be required as long as the actions taken were within the policies of the school. The assistants could keep whatever records they wanted for themselves, but he would no longer review them. He also told them that, if a situation was serious and might lead to a recommendation for expulsion, then he wanted to be in on those cases. However, if the actions were routine, no report would be required.

The response from the assistant principals was one of delight because they had gotten rid of a lot of unnecessary paperwork. They were also grateful for this expression of confidence in them and their ability to make proper decisions. The principal was rewarded because he gained Friday afternoon which he usually devoted to unnecessary duplication of subordinates' work.

He found too that he could delegate a lot of the reading he normally did. If a report or magazine came in pertaining to some curriculum area, for example, he would send it to the departmental chairperson in that curriculum area with a note asking that he be informed of anything new or different that it contained. Instead of papers being stacked up, they were now dispersed as soon as they arrived. The staff members were complimented by the fact that they were asked to keep their leader apprised of new developments in their areas of specialty. The material was read while it was fresh and the principal went about his work knowing he was fully informed of all new developments.

He also found it possible to delegate certain speaking engagements. Organizations would call asking him to appear because of his position as principal. He started sharing these opportunities with assistant principals, counselors, department chairs, etc. When an organization called, he tried to determine what it was they wanted to know about the school. For example, if they wanted to know about the new mathematics program which had been adopted, he would send the math department chairperson. In this way, the organization heard from a specialist instead of getting a second-hand report from a generalist.

School administrators may be reluctant to delegate <u>authority</u> because they fear losing control. (Note the emphasis on authority; responsibility cannot be delegated. The leader is always responsible for everything that happens in an organization.) Monitoring of activities keeps the leader fully informed and in control without his personally performing the tasks. The goal is to use the highest abilities of all our employees by requiring them to do everything of which they are capable. The primary responsibility of leadership is to get the most from people. This also prevents the bottlenecks that can occur when authority is not delegated promptly.

Elementary teachers who are allowed to put students in classes according to their best judgment will study student folders and defend the system with parents. If the principal does the sectioning, it is likely the teachers will complain of the groupings and never study the folders. High-school teachers who help build the master schedule, will make sure it works rather than make it a source of complaints.

Here are some of the benefits that accrue to school leaders when they study and implement the techniques of delegation.

1. *Allows more creative management time.*

To avoid an inundation of paper and instead spend time planning, doing research and other visionary activities, one must be a good delegator. When subordinates are permitted to make decisions, the leader can get out of the office to do more important tasks like motivating staff and discovering new ways of delivering services. If the power focus is mainly on the top hierarchy, the paper will flow that way and so will the pressure. Power <u>and</u> pressure should be shared with the entire staff.

2. *Facilitates staff training and development.*

People learn by doing much more readily than vicariously watching others. As subordinates are allowed to perform tasks, they gain the hands-on experience necessary for mastery. Good delegation is a vital part of an ongoing program of preparing others for greater responsibility.

3. *Increases staff motivation and challenge.*

Employees become excited about their work when they are given ownership. Delegation of authority is a statement of confidence in the subordinate, and it is also highly complimentary. When teachers are given a role in management they commit to the goals they help establish and contribute to the spirit of teamwork.

4. *Increases total productivity.*

Administrators should not be judged by what they do with their own brains and hands. Instead, leaders should be judged by what all of their subordinates do with their intellect and energy. When administrators play proper leadership roles in helping workers identify their talents and high goals and of recognizing subordinates' achievement, the result is that more work is produced as all of the members of the organization make their best contribution.

5. *Provides for recognition and advancement.*

Sharp, clear delegation delineates assignments in such a way that everyone knows exactly who is producing the most. This means those who do the most and best work will get the recognition they deserve and wholesome accountability is achieved. When workers know they will be rewarded for their efforts or identified for their lack of effort in every instance, this inevitability of being noticed rewards those who desire recognition and stimulates those who are tentative.

Why are school administrators in particular reluctant to delegate? Some believe it is because universities do not emphasize this skill. Whatever the reasons, it is a tool that must be mastered either in training or on the job. Administrators must find ways to eliminate whatever impediments stand in the way rather than accept them. Some of the more frequently given reasons for not delegating are:

CHOOSE COMPETENT SUBORDINATES, TRAIN THEM WELL AND THEN DELEGATE FULL AUTHORITY SO THEY CAN DO THEIR BEST FOR THE ORGANIZATION.

• **Fear of subordinates' incompetency.**

When people who work for school leaders are not competent to make decisions, it is the job of the leader to train them until they are competent. During training, mistakes will be made, and this is normal. The important thing is growth will occur, and mistakes will be reduced over time.

After the personnel have been thoroughly trained and given ample opportunity to learn, if they still cannot do high-quality work, they should be replaced. This is due process that satisfies legal requirements and is also quite humane. Nothing would be more unfair than to keep someone in a job that they cannot learn after training and re-training.

• Fear of subordinates' competency.

Some people do not delegate because they are afraid the subordinates will do the work so well that management will suffer by comparison. Others say that if they delegate too much, all of the work will be done at a lower level, and the school board will ask why they need an administrator. The point is that delegation is not done so that leaders have nothing to do; rather it permits leaders to do higher-level tasks as the organization grows and improves. Plus, the one delegating enjoys the enhanced image that comes from empowering the group.

• Subordinates already overworked.

Subordinate overload is often due to redundancy of tasks, overlap of assignments, or just plain lack of planning. Leaders must balance the division of labor to make sure there is no task overlap between employees or creation of unnecessary work. It is possible to have department chairpersons spend their time writing memos to each other with little of it in the interest of the organization. The object is to make sure that priorities are established so that only necessary work is being done and so that the most important tasks are accomplished.

• Loss of control.

Loss of control is an unfounded fear because the leader who does good delegation will be on top of things through monitoring and frequent communication rather than through routines. The leader stays focused on the large picture, reviews outcomes and receives the kind of information which is essential at the executive level.

• Perfectionism.

Staff members should be encouraged to do good work but not to do a job over and over in an attempt to make it perfect. When high goals are set and a large quantity of work completed, improvement is greater than when a job is done repeatedly. Perfectionism is unnecessary and unrealistic. Many people do excellent work but in different ways.

There are two great problems when trying to get an organization to improve delegation up and down the line. The first problem is the myth that the best decisions are made at the top. One can understand how this feeling might exist, but under close scrutiny it is found to be untrue. How could someone at the top of an organization make decisions in an isolated department without having worked in that department? How could the superintendent of schools in a large district give answers about some problem pertaining to an individual school bus route when there are hundreds of buses? To overcome this tendency of pushing things to the top, it must be emphasized that the best decisions can be made when conscientious people are given decision-making authority about the things they work with every day.

Another great problem is the natural tendency of people to "reverse delegate." This situation can be protracted by administrators who get ego reinforcement from having subordinates bring them things to decide. Some managers do not feel they are really managing unless they constantly make decisions. Subordinates must be helped to overcome this natural tendency; they must be made to realize that people who make good decisions are valued over those who carry their problems to their superior.

Some of the techniques and attitudes necessary for effective delegation are as follows:

1. *Delegate fully.*

By delegating fully, it is meant that complete tasks are given to competent subordinates who follow a project from beginning to end and then report results. Subordinates must also be encouraged to delegate to the people who work under them. In this way the decision making is done at the lowest level in the organization.

2. *Gain consensus.*

When someone is given a task to do, they should feel complimented by having authority given to them. This feeling is important for success and it can be delicate to achieve. If someone is assigned a task and they think they are being given it because someone higher up will not condescend to do it, they may feel they have had garbage dumped on them. This will not produce a very enthusiastic worker.

Negative feelings can be avoided if the person giving the assignment discusses with the subordinate the task to be done, and together they set the deadline and structure the task. The decision is made relative to what is to be achieved when the job is finished; the subordinate takes charge, designs the process and does the work. The subordinate has ownership of the task, which eliminates the feeling of doing another person's work.

3. *Stress independence.*

People must be permitted to work independently without having to come frequently for guidance and direction. The subordinate gets full recognition when the work is done well or must live with the results if it is done poorly. This procedure also projects admiration for people who can take the initiative and make decisions with a minimum of supervision.

4. Require organized reports.

Some employees will come in to see the boss with a fragmented or disorganized report rather than clear information and a firm recommendation. If leaders do not exercise care, they can end up assuming the task at this point by helping the person get organized. When this happens, the disorganized person is relieved of responsibility, and the leader is the victim of reverse delegation. If someone submits a disorganized report, he should be asked to take it back until it is organized and all recommendations within it are based upon documented information.

5. Avoid options or alternatives.

Some workers complete a project and then do not like the recommendation they have to make to management. At this point there is a great temptation to bring in several recommendations so that the manager can choose one. This is a tempting way to shed a distasteful job on someone else and avoid making difficult decisions.

If options or alternatives are accepted, the leader must go back and redo the work and make the decision. This also means that one person will take all of the heat for the decision that has to be made. A better way is to diffuse some of that heat throughout the organization by requiring people at every level to take a stand. When someone presents alternatives or options, that person should be asked, "Which one are you recommending? Which one is best?" This tactic causes unnecessary alternatives to disappear because they cannot be used to avoid taking a position.

6. Raise everyone to their highest level of competency.

Our goal is to have employees grow and become everything they are capable of being. The best way to do this is to give them all the authority they are capable of exercising. Then let the superstars take off and those who are not willing or capable are counseled out of the organization. This is leadership at its best.

DELEGATION AND PAPERWORK

People who study delegation are taught to ask themselves certain questions when they make up their list each morning of the things they are going to do that day. As they write an item on the list, they ask themselves, "Must I do this? Can some subordinate do this?" If the answer is that someone else can do it, then that task should be delegated.

It is also suggested that each paper that comes to the desk be handled just once. When the paper arrives, it is either done right then, or if it is not ready for action, sent back immediately. If it is a paper that could be done by someone else, it is delegated and others follow through. If the paper is not important, it is thrown in the trash, rather than retained. This "Do It, Delegate It, or Dump It" approach to paper keeps desks and minds clear of clutter.

For example, if the secretary prepares a letter for the administrator's signature and there is a misspelled word in it, the letter is not accepted because it is not correct. Rather than correcting the error, the leader sends the letter back with a note, "Please correct spelling." The secretary is required to determine which word is misspelled. This emphasizes the importance of having things complete, including words spelled correctly, before they are sent to the administrator's office. This is not a severe or heartless approach to dealing with subordinates because they will feel better about themselves as they grow and realize they are able to perform a high standard of work.

A principal who started traveling a great deal said she would have her secretary make the travel arrangements. Airplane tickets, reservations for hotels and rental cars were secured and placed in a little packet ready for her trip. Before departing, the principal would go through the materials and frequently find an error. This was hard to understand because her secretary was very competent and rarely made mistakes.

Then one day she realized what was causing these mistakes. She was the culprit because she was double checking the secretary's work. The secretary knew the principal was going to look over everything before she started her journey. The principal was not showing full confidence in her secretary. The principal did not recall ever finding another mistake after she announced that she would not longer be able to check these materials before she went traveling. She told the secretary if there was an error it would not be revealed by a second checking. The principal called attention to the importance of the secretary doing the work accurately and thus eliminated the problem and freed herself from having to double check her secretary's work.

How much can emphasis on delegation improve a given situation? A management consultant had a secretary make a note of everything an assistant superintendent did one day in a small school district. This was done without the assistant superintendent's knowledge. When the consultant and assistant superintendent reviewed the list later, they determined that one half of the tasks could have been delegated—a not unusual situation.

CHAPTER SIX
Maximize Meetings

Several national surveys have been done in recent years to determine if meeting time is time well spent. All such surveys have a common finding: about eighty percent of meeting time is wasted time, according to those who attend. The recommendations contained in this chapter are designed to eliminate this demoralizing and expensive situation.

Leaders must constantly evaluate the techniques they are using, so behavior can be validated or modified. A method used frequently is a survey of the opinions of personnel in the organization. Employees are asked to respond to what has happened in the past year, for example, and to make recommendations for improvements to be made in the future. One such survey was done by a special education program director, who asked his teachers and teacher assistants to describe what they liked most and least about their jobs.

The results of the survey were quite predictable because similar outcomes occur in just about every survey of teacher feelings. What they liked best about their job was working with individual students and seeing them progress. What they liked least, often stated with great passion, was the meetings they had to attend.

It is abundantly clear from such samplings of opinion that meetings have a tremendous impact on the morale of an organization. Indeed they can become part of a vicious cycle. A bad meeting makes attendees feel abused, and they go away realizing their time has been wasted. The next time a meeting is announced they go with negative expectations rather than an open mind or eager anticipation. Possible benefits that might have been realized are prevented by the negative attitudes; the meeting is a failure and the cycle is complete. This cycle can be broken if conscious attention is given to good meeting mechanics and to the natural tendencies of people.

The way meetings are held in most organizations reveals interesting phenomena at work. For example, as noted earlier in this book, it is easy to predict which persons are going to be late for a meeting because it is usually those who live the closest. If attendees have to go a great distance to a meeting, they plan ahead, set goals, and arrive early. But if the meeting is nearby, they will take it for granted they will be on time without planning or giving much care.

It is also easy to predict who is going to be late for a meeting because it is usually the same people every time. They are not late because they have had an emergency, since it is unlikely the same people have repeated emergencies. They are late because of their attitude; they do not put a priority on punctuality, and their leaders have permitted this behavior without assessing any consequences.

Chronic tardiness is also encouraged when meetings don't start on time. Attendees realize that when they go on time the meeting usually starts late and they are punished for their promptness. To avoid this punishment they get into the habit of going late and a major time-wasting behavior becomes institutionalized.

Effective leaders can address these situations and turn them from negative to positive by implementing the fundamental changes presented in this chapter. When proper rules are consistently followed, meetings can be made the object of praise by employees, who look forward to and benefit from them because of their high quality.

To achieve these important and positive results most organizations find they must change the way meetings are usually held. For example, a "consent agenda," mentioned previously, can be used to send out in advance written materials containing announcements that do not require discussion. The presider begins the meeting by asking if participants have any questions about the material sent out in advance. If there are no questions, the materials are accepted as distributed. An added benefit of this procedure is that people read with care what is distributed because they know that they will be held accountable for it and there will be no reminders.

Employees are informed that an effort is being made to have fewer and shorter meetings and that meetings will be held only when there is need for discussion. When the staff realizes the goal is to have fewer meetings and shorter meetings, they will be more likely to come on time and with enthusiasm to help achieve these objectives. Their promptness and positive attitude make it possible to get more done in less time, thus establishing a wholesome cycle.

This is another example of how people respond positively to the expectations of leaders. So positive expectations must be underscored to bring positive results. An elementary principal explained how she doubled the attendance at her night meetings by announcing a positive objective. When she sent out the notice about a meeting, she printed in big bold print at the bottom of the announcement that the meeting would start at 7:30 pm and end at 9:00 pm. She added a statement assuring there was no way the meeting would be allowed to extend even one second beyond 9 o'clock. People came in large numbers because they knew that they would not be trapped in a long meeting for which no definite ending time had been established.

A professor who lectures on parenting explained how he drew large crowds. "I let people know exactly what they will get from the meeting. I let them know I will go year by year from prenatal through adolescence telling parents what they should do each year to be effective parents. Then I put on the notice this promise: 'The meeting will start exactly at 7:00 pm and end exactly at 8:00 pm.' "

He said the results are marvelous. "At eight I have covered what I promised and I make sure I never run overtime. I tell the audience they are dismissed but after a ten-minute break, I will take questions for another fifty minutes from any who wishes to stay. Half of them leave, half remain and all are happy. People are grateful for this considerate use of their time."

39

It is also important to remember that meetings are expensive. A technique to demonstrate this is to calculate the average salary of people in a given meeting. Every ten minutes the cost can be totalled and announced. Leaders are often amazed at the cost incurred, and such calculations encourage more careful thought as to the number of meetings that are held.

When it is determined that a meeting is the most appropriate way to handle a situation, the following guidelines should be considered:

1. *Cancel the meeting.*

In education, as in other professions and in business, meetings are often scheduled far in advance to keep the calendars clear. This causes an inherent danger that a meeting will be held just because it has been scheduled. Meetings scheduled far in advance or those that are held on a regular basis such as weekly or monthly must have someone assigned to verify the need. A designated person reviews the situation prior to meeting time and, if there is not a pressing need, a notice is sent to cancel the meeting.

A superintendent related how he found himself getting on the telephone the day before a staff meeting and soliciting items to be presented. "In retrospect, I suspect I was doing this because of my own ego needs," he said. "Being in the spotlight was fun. Our meetings had become pleasant social events. Now I satisfy these needs in a far less expensive way."

2. *Send a subordinate.*

School administrators are invited to a variety of meetings; some are professional meetings in the local school district and some are because of civic responsibility and many are social. It is natural to assume that leaders must attend every meeting to which they are invited. This really is not true. What is needed is someone to represent the organization. To guarantee sufficient time for families and health and to keep from getting spread too thin, school administrators must look upon attendance at these meetings as something that can be shared with other members of the organization.

3. *Distribute an agenda in advance.*

Participants must come to the meeting prepared for action, and this can be achieved by sending out an agenda in advance. Everybody must know what is going to be discussed, so they can bring the necessary materials and so they can give preliminary thought to the matters to be considered.

It is also important to have the beginning and ending times of the meeting listed on the agenda. In this way the participants can plan for a minimum disruption in their own work schedule. If only the beginning time has been listed, it is very difficult for those attending to know when they can resume other activities.

4. *Have the right people attend.*

It is incumbent upon the leader of the meeting to ensure that the people who are called to attend are the ones actually needed. If people are called by job category, then they may be trapped in a session which has no meaning for them. For example, if a notice is sent requiring all school-based secretaries to report to the central office at a given time and no agenda is sent along, it is impossible for the secretaries to know what is to be discussed. All of the secretaries in the schools respond only to find that the discussion has to do only with attendance procedures. The secretaries who work in other departments have to sit through the meeting, even though they have no involvement in attendance.

5. *Prepare the meeting room.*

It can be frustrating to show up for a meeting and find that adequate preparations have not been made. Excuses are made for the audio-visual equipment that is not working properly and someone is sent to look for the handouts that were supposed to be distributed. No amount of excuses make up for the fact that time is wasted. It is imperative that everything be checked in advance so work can begin without delay.

6. *Start on time.*

If meetings always start on time, people will respond by coming on time. If meetings start late, those who come on time are discouraged from doing so in the future. Common sense demands that behavior to be rewarded should be positive, so it will continue to be exhibited.

7. *Never repeat for latecomers.*

When someone comes late to a meeting, there's a great temptation to make sure they are "caught up" by repeating for them the things that have already been discussed. This demoralizes those who came on time when they realize

41

there is no penalty for lateness. Latecomers should be required to be responsible for getting whatever they missed.

It is also a subtle form of reverse delegation if those who come late are able to get the leader to compensate for their tardiness. Therefore, latecomers should not get missed information from the leader. It is more beneficial to the organization if it is understood that those who are late must get the material from another participant and thus make amends by giving extra effort.

8. *Begin the meeting by reviewing the purposes.*

Even if there is an agenda distributed in advance, it is well to take a minute at the beginning of the meeting to review what the meeting is all about. If there is no agenda in advance, then it is absolutely imperative that such a discussion be held. Most people can recall times when they went to a meeting and, ten minutes after it started, the purpose was still a mystery. Nothing productive can come from such a frustrating situation.

If the purpose is not stated at the beginning of the meeting, attendees should ask questions until the purpose is clear. It is even possible that the person who is conducting the meeting is unclear about the purpose. This discussion of objectives, no matter how it's initiated, is absolutely essential for maximum success.

9. *Stay on the agenda.*

It is the job of a leader to see that the agenda is adopted and then followed. Quick review of the agenda at the beginning of the meeting helps focus the attention of the participants. It might even be valuable to set an approximate amount of time for each item on the agenda to keep the group moving and to avoid unnecessary repetition.

If the group starts to wander from the agenda, it is the responsibility of the leader to take action. A take-charge statement such as, "Now we were talking about item number four. What else do we need to do with that item?" This statement should stop the wandering and bring people back to the agenda.

If an individual brings up an extraneous point, the leader might say something like, "That is a topic that we need to discuss but since it doesn't fit in with today's agenda, let's make a note of it for a future time." A gentle firmness on the part of the leader is essential to keep the group on target.

10. *Control participants.*

The needs of the group must always be superior to the needs of the individuals attending the meeting, and this situation can only be maintained by an astute leader. Individuals must be guided into a spirit of cooperation and be kept from doing things that would be individually satisfying but not in the best interests of the group. The challenge for the leader is to maintain control of the participants without offending.

People come to meetings to satisfy different conscious and subconscious needs. Some look upon the meeting as a social event, a chance to enjoy being with other people. Some would like to make the meeting a place they can monopolize by doing most of the talking. Some like to use meetings for debate with others who hold different views, while some come to rest and be involved as little as possible. The skilled leader controls the behavior of individuals and channels the energy into what is best for the group. For example, if Sam has been talking too much and Susie has not been participating, the next time Sam speaks up, the leader could say something like, "Sam, could you hold that thought for just a moment? We haven't heard from Susie on this point." Sam should get the message that he's talking too much, and Susie should realize she's not participating enough.

11. *Maintain a proper meeting environment.*

Any interruption to a meeting causes a loss of communication for all involved. The simple idea of putting a sign on the door that reads "Meeting in Progress" will reduce interruptions. If someone is going to have to leave the meeting early, an announcement of this fact at the beginning will greatly reduce the interruption when that person leaves. If no announcement is made, every person in the group will ponder the reason for the early exit and, in reality, the meeting has stopped.

The proper environment demands a room free from distractions such as noise or uncovered windows through which activities can be seen. Temperature and lighting should be given careful consideration, and participants should not be crowded together. Seating should neither be uncomfortable nor too comfortable, and there should be a "No Smoking" sign. If printed material is projected on a screen, the letters should be bold and sharp and easily read from anywhere in the room.

12. *The final question: "What did we accomplish?"*

Productivity is enhanced when the people who attend our meetings know that the last question will always be "What did we accomplish?" They anticipate this question as the meeting progresses and work hard to make the answer something positive. A positive response rewards those who worked hard and also defines the next steps to be taken. The minutes of the meeting should contain the summary statement, which evolves as the question of "What was accomplished?" is answered.

13. *Special considerations for large meetings.*

Thus far the discussion has been about guidelines appropriate for meetings where participants can discuss, ask questions and exchange ideas. Often in the educational profession, people are required to participate in large gatherings such as conventions. While these are not meetings in the sense discussed to this point, it is of value to consider how conventions could be improved. This can be done by simply addressing the most frequent complaints that are heard.

When the convention program morning schedule lists one speaker after another with no break from 9:00am until noon, it is obvious there is going to be a problem. People will have to take restroom breaks, so there will be constant movement of people in and out of the auditorium during the speeches. Breaks long enough to accommodate the size of the audience must be scheduled about every hour to prevent this disruption. When convention planners say they do not schedule breaks because they are afraid the audience will not return, the answer is to have more exciting sessions and people will come. If the audience has to be trapped, then something is wrong with the program.

Exhibits should be closed during the general sessions, and ushers should make sure there are not gatherings of people creating noise at the doorways or in the halls during sessions.

At a luncheon or dinner meeting, meal service, including coffee refills, should be completely stopped during a speech. Any movement within the room will distract the audience and make it difficult for the speaker to project emotion, an essential part of any good speech.

Presenters at a convention must be controlled, so they do not exceed their scheduled speaking time, which is unfair to the audience and to other speakers. At some conventions the speaker's microphone is turned off after a warning of two minutes and a second warning of one minute. This is a very effective technique because speakers know they cannot ignore their deadlines.

There are many details to be considered when planning a convention or a large inservice workshop. Most of these details simply require the use of common sense. The convention must be well organized, the schedule crisply maintained, and the needs of the audience considered. This will enhance the enthusiasm of all involved and prevent disappointment and stress. Attention to these details will increase the value of the experience for the organization sponsoring the activity and for the individuals who attend.

CHAPTER SEVEN
Empower Secretaries

School administrators generally have a high opinion of the competencies and possible contributions of educational secretaries. Jokes, which have some substance in fact, are made about how schools can run without difficulty when school administrators are away, but everything comes to a halt when the secretaries are absent. In spite of the fact that secretaries are held in high esteem, they are rarely engaged in a way that makes maximum use of their talents. Instead only menial or clerical tasks are assigned to them.

Educational secretaries, particularly those working in individual schools, are often responsible to the entire faculty rather than just the principal or assistant principal. In these cases, the administrator must establish ground rules to help implement the empowering ideas presented here. All who look to the secretary for service must understand the rules to prevent this valuable person from being caught in conflicting expectations of various staff members. Some of the concepts to follow will need to be customized to fit the reality of any given situation, but in all cases, the goal is to properly engage and direct the work of the secretary so as to save time for everyone.

There is an abundance of evidence suggesting that people work best when they are challenged to use their highest abilities. Thus, it would seem wise to elevate the expectations of what the secretary can contribute, and to do this it is necessary to break the widely held stereotypical view that a secretary can only do clerical tasks. Because of this prevailing view in many schools and offices secretaries are not allowed to exercise initiative or go beyond carrying out specific directives.

A new and enlightened role for the secretary permits this valuable person to become an extension of the leadership and to act within the scope of generalized authority. The secretary makes decisions based upon the parameters of the school's authority and established policies. Instead of waiting for permission to do anything above and beyond the simplest chore, an elevated role is assigned where the secretary becomes a full member of the team.

Such use of the secretary is often met with reluctance by school administrators. They fear that giving such authority to the secretary will cause problems with teachers and with other administrators. However, there are many instances where positive relationships exist among all categories of personnel even though the secretary is being used in this enlightened way. Obviously, such changes of assignment must be made gradually, and the secretary must be taught to play the proper role without offending other staff members. This can be accomplished if the administrator and the secretary consciously move into these new territories cautiously and with sensitivity to the feelings of all people in the organization.

In other words, this change of role for the educational secretary should be done in an evolutionary rather than a revolutionary manner. As success is experienced in assigning authority to this new team member, then ways are found to delegate even more authority. The goal is to determine the highest potential of the individual so that the greatest contribution can be made. This constant search for maximum potential helps break the stereotypical view mentioned earlier as a prime cause for the underutilization of secretaries.

This perspective on the secretarial contribution also causes employers to look for different qualities in a candidate for this position. There was a time when speed of typing, shorthand skills and filing were emphasized. These are no longer given as much consideration but instead, more attention is directed toward personal qualities such as poise, maturity and excellent people skills. The successful candidate should be self-motivated and dedicated to making a success of every assignment. A person with these and similar qualities will quickly master any technical skills necessary for doing a superb job; they will learn what they need to know and they will do it quickly. Excellent technical skills will never compensate for a lack of maturity or for an abrasive personality.

After the person with these personal qualities has been selected, then a job description should evolve. The word *evolve* is used to indicate that the teammates working together develop the specifics of the working relationship. The administrator plays the leading role and has the last word, but the secretary and administrator work as equal partners in deciding who will do certain tasks.

Starting with a general understanding of assignments, the specific details are developed as the work progresses and as each job is approached for the first time. The administrator and the secretary together decide whose job it is. When the same task is undertaken in the future, responsibility remains with the same individual and requires no further consideration unless one of the team proposes a change.

The basic goal for the relationship of the office team is simple but crucial to success. The goal of the secretary is to do everything possible to make the administrator look great; the goal of the administrator is to do everything possible to make the secretary look great. Nothing adversarial must creep into the relationship in any way.

PUBLIC RELATIONS

The secretary is ordinarily the first contact with people over the telephone or in person as they visit the office. As someone observed, "You never get a second chance to make a first impression." Thus, encountering a school's secretary is crucial to the school's ongoing public image.

The secretary who operates the switchboard in a school or school district is a key person when it comes to public relations. Callers must experience a helpful person who always has a smile in the voice, someone who seems eager to receive

46

A MAJOR GOAL OF THE SECRETARY IS TO DO EVERYTHING POSSIBLE TO MAKE THE ADMINISTRATOR LOOK GREAT!
A MAJOR GOAL OF THE ADMINISTRATOR IS TO DO EVERYTHING POSSIBLE TO MAKE THE SECRETARY LOOK GREAT!

---

the call. The caller must feel as a welcomed guest would feel in a home. The switchboard operator must never project tension, agitation or anything that would indicate the caller is an intruder. This test should be used for training of switchboard operators and others who receive phone calls, namely, "Every person who calls this office must have a higher opinion of this office after they call, no matter why they call, even if they call with a complaint." This is a severe test, but one which pays dividends when its objectives are met.

When someone enters the office, this person must be greeted immediately with a smile. A visitor must never be made to wait while a secretary finishes a project such as taking a telephone call. If the visitor cannot be served immediately, the secretary must look up, smile, and say something like, "I'll be with you in a minute." The absence of an immediate greeting causes tension, just as when a customer enters a store and has to wait to be acknowledged.

Public relations will be enhanced if the secretary knows how to reduce anger in callers. For example, if someone phones a school and is angry at the principal, anything the principal says in retort will probably increase the anger of the caller. But the secretary has a unique opportunity to reduce the anger before the call is forwarded to the administrator. The caller is not mad at the secretary, which means the secretary can play an intervening role to sooth the angry person.

When a secretary senses that a caller is angry, the following three-step process can be employed to reduce the anger:

A. *Always agree with the angry caller.*

This is not to suggest that the secretary should agree with what the angry person is saying, but rather, to do something which meets the emotional needs being expressed by the angry person. The secretary can say something like, "I'm so sorry

47

you're upset. Please let me help you." This does not imply that the angry caller is correct; it only announces an eagerness to help, which is likely to reduce anger.

B. *Listen.*

Listening with sympathy to the angry caller, without evaluating the statements made will usually cause anger to subside. Listening reduces anger, and time is not wasted because it will probably prevent more phone calls that would have been made if the angry caller had experienced curt treatment.

C. *Underscore and elevate anything positive which the angry caller says.*

For example, if the angry caller says, "Until three weeks ago I was pleased with your service," then the secretary can say something like, "Please give us a chance to get things back the way they were three weeks ago because we want you to be happy with our service."

When these steps are successfully taken, and the secretary forwards to the administrator a caller who is no longer angry, a great service has been performed for the team. It is likely that the caller will say to the administrator something like, "I was angry when I called your office but because your secretary was so understanding I'm no longer angry. That is really a great secretary that you have." The caller is right, because a thoroughly educated, professional secretary acted in the best interest of the entire building's team.

OFFICE MANAGER

It is recommended that all administrators implement a step-by-step process where the secretary takes over everything having to do with day-to-day running of the office. The secretary manages the schedules for both members of the team. The secretary makes sure the administrator leaves in time to get to meetings promptly and manages the tickler file to see that forms are returned on time and that the mail is handled expeditiously.

Administrators should not carry an appointment book. If someone asks for an appointment, the administrator simply refers them to the secretary, who keeps the schedule of appointments. This prevents conflicts and also allows the secretary to screen and set priorities.

CONFIDENTIAL COUNSELOR

The administrator-secretary relationship is a mutually supportive one where each is dedicated to the welfare of the other: two people who share similar goals and who succeed as a partnership. Someone once described this relationship as two people sharing one job.

The wise school administrator will make full use of this professional relationship. When decisions are made, the secretary is consulted and the judgment of this person is valued. Secretaries are away from the organization less frequently than administrators and tend to have a better feel about the mood of staff members. People tend to be more candid with the secretary in contrast to the leader of the organization.

This is not to suggest in any way that the secretary should be used as a spy or informer on other staff members. This would have negative consequences and would inhibit normal relationships between the secretary and other employees. It does recognize that the first loyalty of the secretary is to the administrator. It does not entail being disloyal to others in the organization. It means that the administrator will look to the secretary to help assess moods and themes that relate to the overall morale in the school or office. The astute secretary also will apprise administration of any developing problem areas. In summary, the secretary is an excellent sounding board to inform and enlighten the administrator.

SPECIFIC GUIDELINES FOR THE RELATIONSHIP

There are guidelines which can be used to strengthen the administrator-secretary relationship. The list presented here is by no means exhaustive but should be thought of as illustrative of things a leader can do to empower the secretary.

1. *Start off on the right foot.*

When a secretary is hired or when an administrator starts a new job where a secretary is already in place, it is well to have a discussion before work begins. This discussion is to set a positive tone by letting the secretary know that the office will be run in a spirit of cooperation and that the role of secretary is looked upon as a very important one. The discussion held before the two begin to work together is the one opportunity each will have to announce their mutual expectations without offending.

When a new secretary is hired, the conversation prior to employment might be something like the following (after the two have pretty well made up their minds they want to work together). The administrator might begin by saying, "May I ask you some personal questions? I want to be sure that if we work together we will be happy. You can feel free to ask me any questions which you have in mind."

The candidate gives permission and then the administrator begins to announce his or her expectations. The dialogue might go something like this:

"If you get this job, will you ever be late for work?"

The candidate may reply, "I'm an early riser; I get my clothes organized the night before so I'm rarely late. Since I know how important this is to you, I would give special care to punctuality."

"Very good. And how about personal phone calls? Will you be receiving personal phone calls here at the office?"

"We get organized early in the morning so the need for personal calls would be infrequent."

"Will you ever gossip?"

"I understand confidentiality. I don't gossip."

After about the third question, the candidate can then begin to ask questions and the first one is usually "If I get this job will you ever leave the office without telling me where you are going and how long you're going to be gone?"

A wise administrator will likely be pleased to make such a commitment because it is good office practice.

The second question might be "If I get this job, will you start taking me for granted or will you compliment me for good work and extra effort?" A commitment here should be no problem for a leader who knows the value of praise deserved.

These discussions before the working relationship begins will pay dividends as long as two people are working together. It is a conversation that can only be held at this time because, after a person is employed, discussion about these and similar matters comes across as criticism.

2. *Build self-esteem.*

Some secretaries have their own stereotyped view of what their role should be. They see themselves as mainly clerical workers and are reluctant to take on what seem to them management duties. In these situations it is necessary to point out the abilities they possess and that opportunity will be given to use all of their abilities. The operating mode of the office will be such that one person has ultimate responsibility, but two people exercise the authority that stems from the leader's position. It should be made very clear that the reward for excellent work will be greater freedom for the secretary and more opportunity to grow. There will be no artificial limitations imposed by a job title or by practices from the past.

3. *Work as a team.*

For best results the office should operate as a team. This means that the secretary and the administrator work together, but they don't work on the same tasks at the same time. There is frequent communication but little overlap in what they do. For example, the administrator establishes the ground rules for scheduling appointments. The secretary then administers the scheduling of appointments according to the guidelines established. When someone calls to schedule an appointment with the administrator, the secretary gives an immediate answer without having to check with the administrator or without having the caller wait for an answer.

4. *Let the secretary plan.*

In some schools and offices the secretary is used as a personal aide to the administrator. This means that little planning can be done because the secretary's main obligation is to be constantly available to respond to the whim of the leader. It is imperative that leaders become more sensitive to how difficult it is to plan when one does not know from one minute to the next what must be done. More planning together will reduce interruptions to the secretary's schedule.

5. *See the secretary first.*

It is recommended that the secretary and administrator hold a brief meeting first thing each morning. They decide which tasks must be done that day and which are assigned to the administrator and which to the secretary. They get each other organized and then they work independently of each other as much as possible. This means each can plan the day's activities without a great danger of being interrupted by the teammate.

6. *Let the secretary screen.*

Everything (and everybody) entering the office must come to the secretary first. Only in this way can priorities be set and maintained, and interruptions minimized. In any organization there will always be some who want to circumvent the secretary. The leader must act firmly and swiftly to keep this behavior from becoming a serious problem.

7. *The secretary handles the mail.*

The administrator should be involved in mail handling as little as possible. The secretary is given authority to throw away junk mail, reroute mail to other offices, and then prepare letters for the administrator's signature. This procedure avoids time wasters such as dictation, transcription and reading of junk mail.

8. *The secretary controls all phone calls.*

When secretaries are given authority to handle phone calls from beginning to end, many calls can be handled without further transfer. Telephoning can be delegated so that phone calls go from secretary to secretary, and one can virtually eliminate call-back slips and telephone tag. The secretary can block calls politely, find out what the caller wants, and provide the information. Thus, calls can become a one-person task rather than having the secretary answer and then pass the caller on to someone else in the office. It is imperative that the secretary be well informed, so that as many phone calls as possible are handled by the person who originally answers the phone.

9. *The secretary manages visitors.*

Ground rules should be established for the secretary's role when greeting visitors—those with and without appointments. Techniques for determining what unannounced visitors want and then referring them to more appropriate offices are important and should be established. Great stress is placed upon making a good first impression on all visitors.

10. *Office routines are secretarial prerogatives.*

Rules should be established for all routines such as machinery repair and supervision of custodial services. The secretary then follows through and involves the administrator only with periodic updates and when unusual situations arise.

In summary,, the importance of the secretary as described here demands that this person possess excellent personal qualities. "People skills" are essential. In light of this, the past record of the candidate should be carefully investigated when a new secretary is chosen. The pace of new technology will continue to accelerate, so computer knowledge and a willingness to continue learning in this area are mandatory. This secretary should also be given inservice training as are teachers and other professional staff members.

CHAPTER EIGHT

Block Interruptions

An organizational skills workshop was held for a group of school principals, and one participant was having a particularly hard time buying the idea that a schedule would improve her day. She said, "I've tried making a schedule and it just doesn't work for me. It seems inevitable that interruptions destroy my plans. I can't just turn people away when they need me."

The instructor tried as gently as possible to suggest that she may be making herself more vulnerable than necessary and that she might try taking projects off to a conference room and let only the secretary be aware of her whereabouts. "See if they won't solve some of the problems themselves as they do when you are away," he said. He also recommended that she close her door for periods of time, so she could avoid visitors except in case of real emergencies.

She still did not seem persuaded so the instructor concluded by suggesting, "Any day we have a schedule we will be better off than when we don't have a schedule even if we are interrupted. And, if the interruptions continue after we have tried to manage our time, perhaps it would be wise to schedule a chunk of time to handle interruptions." She finally seemed persuaded by the logic, adding, "If I set aside a chunk of time for interruptions and none occur, I'll do one of my standby tasks." Insight replaced her initial skepticism and she became enthusiastic about learning more about reducing interruptions as a way of saving time.

Interruptions can be a constant reality unless there is sensitivity to what constitutes an interruption and the impact they can have. The counselor in a high school called a student to his office by using the public address system. He apparently did not consider that all work stopped for the rest of the students in that class for a period of several minutes. It has been estimated that four minutes of education is lost for every student in school when an announcement is made using the public address system!

It is quite unpleasant to have a meal or home activity interrupted by an untimely telephone call. School administrators need time away from the job and freedom from calls at home in order to maintain their mental health; steps must be taken to prevent these interruptions in the evenings and on weekends. For example, other staff members could be asked to take turns being "on-call," and more information can be made available by voice mail, telephone answering machines, or E-mail.

The best way to deal with interruptions is to have systems in place to prevent them. For example, most administrators learned in college they should have an "Open-Door" policy. This statement is often misinterpreted; it does not mean that administrators may never close the door and must be constantly available to other people no matter what the priority of the contact. It means that those who work in the organization can reach the leader when necessary through a system often referred to as a "Variable Door" system. When the door is closed, this signals only urgent items will be received. When the door is open, more casual contacts are permitted.

SOME ACTIVITIES LOOK LIKE LEGITIMATE EXPENDITURES OF TIME BUT ARE ACTUALLY INTERRUPTIONS IN DISGUISE.

The principal who makes contact with his teachers first thing in the morning on a regular basis by being in the halls and where teachers congregate will eliminate the need for many interruptions. The teachers know they have a chance to talk with him or her every morning. An elementary principal said she ate in different lunch periods each day so that in a few days she would lunch with all her teachers. "This had the effect of eliminating the need for teachers to come to my office unless they had something confidential to discuss."

A superintendent of schools had a similar technique which was effective in reducing interruptions by principals who came to his office. He held a monthly luncheon meeting with each category of administrators who worked for him. The first Monday of each month he met with the high-school principals. The second Monday was devoted to the junior high principals, and the third Monday was spent with the elementary school principals. On the fourth Monday of each month a session with the central office personnel was scheduled.

The ground rules for these meetings were very simple: there would be no agenda, no presentation by the superintendent or his staff. It was strictly a session to get together and talk about anything that surfaced, anything on the minds of the subordinate administrators. He found a lot of his time was spent debunking rumors.

Interruptions must first be recognized as time wasters and then dealt with in a positive way. The checklist below was designed to address the major time wasters of school administrators.

1. *Most interruptions look legitimate.*

Two people are sitting in an office talking and it appears they are having a business conference. Upon closer investigation it is discovered that it is not a business conference at all. One person was sitting in the office with the door open, and another came by and just dropped in. Instead of a planned conference with an objective in mind, the occupant of the office became the victim of a drop-in visitor.

54

An in-basket stacked high with papers sitting on someone's desk might seem quite legitimate. In reality, an in-basket on the desk becomes a distraction because items in it catch a person's attention. It becomes even more of a distraction if it becomes a repository for other people's priorities. An uncontrolled in-basket provides an easy way for other people to dump their problems and impose their priorities.

Some people leave their office doors open so that they will appear to be approachable and available to colleagues and subordinates. On the surface it seems to be a legitimate way to achieving these goals, but in reality the open door becomes an invitation for everybody to come in at any time, no matter what the priority of their visit. When a person is in an office and the door is open, she should not face the door. It is better to turn so that her side or even back is to the door.

2. *Have set reception hours.*

Subordinates need to know when leaders are available to them or they may come at inopportune times and interrupt work on a high-priority item. Such interruptions can be prevented if leaders signal when they are available. For example, the committee chairperson tells the members of the committee the time of the evening when telephone calls will be welcomed. The school principal tells the teachers that he does not want them to make a trip to the office and find him gone. Therefore, he will be available each day from 3:30 to 4:30. Teachers, being busy people, don't want to make a trip and find the principal gone, so they keep in mind the times when the principal is available.

An elementary principal tells her teachers she wants to visit their classes one hour each month to collect data for staff evaluations. "I will come unannounced later in the semester, but the first two visits are your choice; I want to come when it is best for you. Any day of the week except Friday will be fine because I'm reserving that for uninterrupted office time." This principal showed respect for the staff while at the same time reserving Friday for personal use. These teachers know the principal will be unavailable on Friday.

3. *Use signs.*

Interruptions in offices and other work places often occur because people come in to ask questions that could just as easily be answered by a sign posted in the lobby. If a special meeting is being held in a building on a given day, a sign should be put up that morning directing people to the meeting so they do not have to come into the office to ask directions. A good locator board placed in the lobby of the building telling people how to find certain offices and functions will get people where they want to go without their having to inquire.

4. *Let the secretary screen.*

As recommended earlier, the secretary and the administrator operate as a team, and the secretary is the one who makes first contact with the outside world. Everything that comes into the office must go through the secretary, so proper office priorities can be maintained. The secretary makes decisions on which telephone calls will be put through and what appointments will be scheduled. The administrator must cooperate by insuring that the secretary is not circumvented.

5. *Meet visitors outside.*

Quite frequently after the day has been scheduled someone very important comes in without an appointment. This person cannot very well be turned away without offending, but the extent of the interruption can be minimized. When an unexpected visitor must be seen, the secretary takes that person to another place such as a conference room, so that he or she can be met there instead of the office. This signals that the administrator is very busy, and it underscores the importance of this visitor. The visitor ideally realizes the administrator was busy but took the time anyway. Chances are the visitor will be sensitive about keeping the meeting short.

Most visitors should be met outside the office door, even if they do have an appointment. When the secretary announces that a certain person has arrived, the answer is, " Okay, I'll be right out." When persons are met outside the door, it is found that most people just want to ask a brief question or make a statement and, as soon as they do, are on their way. If it is necessary to have the person come inside to meet in private (and few do), this decision can be made. The important thing is that a conscious decision will be made concerning who will come into the office.

6. *Come to work early.*

On occasion, all people will have to extend the workday beyond the normal working hours. When this is necessary, the tendency is for administrators to stay late at work. When this is done, people come by and interrupt. They are curious and they have no particular plans for their time so they stop by to see what the leader is doing.

If the workday is extended, it is better to leave work on time and then come to work extra early the next morning. There will be few interruptions since not many people are going to set their alarms early to come down to the office because they are curious about what might be going on. (This fact may also indicate the relative importance of their visit.)

7. *Go to the subordinate's office.*

If it is necessary to talk to a subordinate on some minor matter, the tendency is to call that person into the office. Then there is the problem of pushing them out the door when the routine matter is handled. This often leads to extended conversation in the name of courtesy.

A good way to avoid this is to go to the subordinate's office when there is a matter to be handled. The leader can go to the subordinate, take care of the situation, and leave. It seems perfectly comfortable, and no one is offended by the shortness of the visit.

8. *Set time limits.*

Most things take the amount of time they are permitted, so time expenditures can be reduced by setting limits. If work is going to be done on the agenda tomorrow from 9:00 to 9:30, it is best to set a deadline on that effort. The item on the "To Do" list would read, "*Complete* the agenda for the meeting," rather than simply "*work* on" the agenda for the meeting. In this way an individual can set deadlines on his own activities.

It is also important time limits be set for other people. When a visitor is being escorted to the conference table, the host might look at a clock and say something like "I've set aside from now until 10:30 for our meeting. Will that give sufficient time?" The visitor will probably look at his or her watch and say, "Sure, that will be enough time." The result is that both people will work toward the deadline which has been stated.

The secretary should enforce the daily schedule by ringing the phone when someone has been in the office for a stated amount of time. This keeps the administrator from losing track of time and maintains the daily agenda.

9. *Stand-up meetings.*

Sit-down meetings are always much longer than stand-up meetings, so it is important that stand-up meetings be used where appropriate, particularly for a small group. At first it may seem unnatural because stand-up meetings may have rarely been used in the past. But after a while people adjust to the procedure and actually prefer these shorter meetings.

10. *Keep conversation moving.*

When someone comes into the office, the tendency is for the conferees first to discuss extraneous matters rather than get right down to business. While it is beneficial to have some exchange of pleasantries, these should not go beyond a brief period. To get conversation started, a statement such as "What would you like to talk about?" or, "What can I do for you?" will usually cause people to get down to business and talk about what they came to discuss.

If the visitor starts to wander after making the presentation, the leader can say something like, "What is the next step?" or, "Where do we go from here?" These simple statements, inserted into the conversation, will keep people on task.

Phrases that can be used to wrap up or conclude conversations include, "What is your recommendation?" or "How can we summarize what we have discussed?" or "Here is what I understand we have decided."

11. *Signal people to leave.*

When the meeting has been concluded, if the visitor does not leave, body language can be used to signal that it is time to go. The leader can push back from the desk or place the palms of the hands flatly on the desk and rise slowly. When this is done, the visitor rises too. Once he is on his feet, the leader walks toward the door and the visitor follows.

In an office setting people are easier to manage when they are standing rather than sitting. It might be a good idea to have no chairs in front of the desk. If it is decided that sitting is appropriate, a chair can be gotten or they can be invited into the conversation area. If they are standing when they finish their business, it is likely they will leave promptly without extending their visit unnecessarily.

12. *A proper telephone procedure.*

In many offices, when a call comes from the outside it rings both the secretary's phone and the administrator's phone. In some cases the administrator's phone does not ring but a light will flash. This can be distracting because it breaks the train of thought. Even if the call is handled by the secretary without involving anyone else, it is more advantageous to have a telephone system where only one person hears the ring or sees the flashing light. If the secretary has to leave the office unattended, a simple forwarding code will cause the phone to ring somewhere else temporarily.

13. *Be out.*

There will be times when administrators are working on tasks so important that interruptions must be avoided except in the most urgent of circumstances. At these times it is best to get away from the office and go to a conference room or other secluded place to give 100 percent concentration to that task. Only the secretary will know where the administrator is, and instructions will be left that interruptions will be permitted only in the case of an emergency or a very high-priority situation. In this instance the secretary can honestly say that the person is out.

14. *Be sensitive of subordinates' time.*

Administrators at all levels must realize that subordinates will not object to a superior's interruptions. Because of this leaders must be very sensitive and careful to set a good example by being considerate of subordinates' time and the need for all people to enjoy a schedule free of unnecessary interruptions.

CHAPTER NINE

Master the Telephone

The telephone was originally designed to be a servant, but in many cases it has become the master. The challenge with this tool is the same as with many inventions; its benefits must be exploited without incurring the problems that result if it is improperly used. The telephone has become such a part of the culture that it can be taken for granted and little thought given to analyzing its effectiveness. The potential of the telephone as a timesaver can be overlooked and it can also cause the unwary user to fall into time-wasting traps. This chapter suggests ways to avoid such traps and utilize the telephone in the most effective way.

TELEPHONE USE IN SCHOOLS

It is helpful to start by taking a critical look at some of the things done in most organizations relative to the telephone. For example, if one were to eavesdrop on some of the non-personal calls, at least a third of the typical conversations would be found devoted to extraneous matters such as health, office gossip, sports and the weather. It would also be revealed that telephone calls are allowed to interrupt business discussions. When two people are conversing, the telephone rings and immediately the person on the phone is given priority over the conference which was in progress.

Administrators often become victims of the telephone even at home. Family activities are interrupted to answer a call from someone who has the wrong number or even to listen to unsolicited sales pitches. Some have the audacity to expect people to listen to a sales pitch by a robot! It is quite clear that at home or at work, careful attention must be given to the proper utilization of this ubiquitous tool.

In the school setting, it is especially important that the significance of the telephone not be underestimated. A national survey was done some years ago to determine what caused schools and school districts to have certain images. Citizens were asked how they had developed the opinions they held about the schools. Many factors were identified, but a relative few were found to be of paramount importance. The most important factor was what the children said when they went home from school. The second most important item was what the employees of the school district said when they were interacting with the people of the community. The third most important item was the way telephones were managed in the school district. For example, it was found that more people whose children attended an elementary school knew the name of the secretary than the name of the principal — because the secretary answered the telephone. Thus, the secretary and telephone combine to comprise a large percentage of a school district's public relations program.

There is potentially much to be gained when all staff members are educated to the importance of good public relations and the role that the telephone plays in that program. If the telephone is used properly it will make friends for the school and save time, or if used improperly, lose community support and create additional work. A true example will illustrate the point.

A new and very green assistant principal was working at a large junior high school. One of his major assignments was to handle discipline and to interact with the parents in that regard. One day a man called to say that someone had broken into his son's locker and stolen his textbooks. The inexperienced assistant principal immediately tried to set the parent straight. He explained that students in junior high school often share their locker combinations with their friends. He also mentioned that the boy's locker was near the cafeteria and other students often leave their books there rather than going to their own lockers. He was trying to reassure him that the books were not stolen and that they would likely be found soon.

To his surprise, the parent's response was, "You're calling me a liar, aren't you?" When the books were found and the assistant principal called the father, he thought he would be pleased. Instead, he said, "You could have found the books a lot sooner if you hadn't been so busy calling me a liar."

It soon became clear that the way he conveyed information over the telephone made a lot of difference in his effectiveness and in his public image. After this unhappy experience, if a parent called to say that books were missing, instead of trying to correct their thinking, he showed shock and sympathy. "I'm sorry this happened," he said. "Rest assured we don't take theft of books lightly. I will get the police on this immediately."

This sympathetic, nonconfrontational approach produced interesting results. When the parent realized the assistant principal was concerned even to the point of calling the police, the adversarial tone left his voice. His response was something like this, "Before you call the police, you better know what my son is like. Why, he would lose his head if it wasn't attached to him. Besides, he's been giving his locker combination to all his friends and his locker is down by the cafeteria where they all store their books during lunch. Actually, I doubt that the books were stolen. He probably just lost them."

What a difference when this parent was called and told the books had been found. He was so grateful and complimentary of the school's efforts; the assistant principal had gained a friend. What's more important, because of the impact of such incidents on public relations, the school now had a firm supporter.

Educational institutions are learning what sales-oriented businesses have known for many years. The first contact made in person or by telephone establishes an image that has a lingering effect on future relationships. The quality of first impressions must be given priority consideration. For example, if the switchboard operator or receptionist is absent, a veteran employee should replace that

61

person rather than a temporary employee. Temporary employees can be assigned to positions where there is less likelihood of public contact.

In secondary schools, it is a common practice to put students on the switchboard. This is fine if the students are thoroughly educated, motivated, and fulfil the criteria for meeting the public. They must not be placed on the switchboard just because they have been removed from a classroom for misbehavior. Individuals who represent the school as receptionists or telephone operators must be highly skilled and thoroughly trained to deal with the public in the most positive way.

Here are two tests: phone operators must be so thoroughly prepared that they can take a vague request for information and get it to the right office or person the very first time. They must be able to implement the goal which was stated previously that *"Every person who calls this office (or comes into the office) must have a higher opinion of the office after they call, no matter why they call, even if they call with a complaint."*

Being sensitive to the emotions projected over the telephone is a key to favorable public relations. It is fine for voice mail to be used, if the menu is brief and clear and if the voice that delivers information is upbeat and energetic. Of course, it is always better when a human being delivers information instead of a machine. Any time an answering device is used to replace an upbeat, cheerful human being, some loss can be expected.

There are some delicate situations where a machine should never be used. For example, if the school has a device which calls all absentee students every day, there is great danger of offending, especially if the machine calls the parents at work. It may be more advisable to have the calling done by a clerk or even a volunteer student who has been thoroughly trained, even if this means a sampling of absentees on a random basis rather than calling all absentees.

School administrators must know how to make the telephone a positive factor when dealing with the public and also emphasize how telephone mistakes can be prevented. They must know how to defend themselves against telephone intrusion, so others will not impose on their time. They have to be sensitive to what is happening with both incoming and outgoing calls to themselves and to all of the offices in the school or building.

The goal for incoming calls is to always have callers feel good after their call, no matter what the purpose of the call. Just having such a goal in the minds of all staff members and calling attention to it periodically seem to do a great deal of good. This puts everyone on the staff in a helping, sensitive mood even when the person who calls us is upset. It keeps everyone from being curt and helps the staff keep a smile in the voice at all times. There is nothing to be gained by leaving someone with a negative feeling.

The goal for outgoing calls is to convey information in a pleasant way that does not waste other people's time. This type of consideration is appreciated and enhances the chances the next call will be received positively and with fewer attempts at evasion.

OUR GOAL:

"EVERY PERSON WHO CALLS THIS OFFICE MUST HAVE A HIGHER OPINION OF THIS OFFICE AFTER THEY CALL — NO MATTER WHY THEY CALL."

With the understanding that the telephone is the primary public relations instrument in most offices, the following suggestions are offered to maintain a positive image while saving time.

1. *Use the telephone to reduce travel.*

Before making any trip the question should be asked, "Could this matter be handled over the telephone?" If the answer is yes, then the telephone is used rather than making a trip. It is estimated that the average person can save several hours a week just by making this one behavior adjustment.

2. *Place own calls.*

The following is a frequent occurrence in most offices: the telephone rings and a pleasant voice inquires if a certain person is there. "Yes, this is he," comes the reply. Then the caller says, "Would you please hold for_____?" The person being called is then put in the position of holding the telephone for someone who placed the call. Such persons obviously do not realize that they have inadvertently insulted the person whom they have called. This can be avoided, and time can be saved when administrators develop the habit of placing their own outgoing calls. An exception to this would be when the administrator is calling a subordinate.

3. *Who may I say is calling?*

When someone telephones an office, and the secretary says, "Who's calling?" this implies that they must find out if the caller is important enough to have the call received. This is a public relations faux pas. A better way to ask the question and to receive the same information is to ask, "Who may I say is calling?"

4. *May I help you?*

When someone calls and the secretary asks, "May I help you?" the tendency is for the caller to say no in the hopes of speaking to someone higher up. A better question is, "How may I help you?" In this way the caller will reveal the purpose of the call, and often the secretary can say, "I have that information. Let me give it to you." This screens calls without giving the caller the option of bypassing the secretary.

5. *Block calls politely.*

Calls can be screened without offending the caller if the proper techniques are used. The secretary can use a polite technique which determines the priority of the call. For example, when the telephone rings, she answers by giving the name of the office, her name, and then says, "How may I help you?" The caller then says she wants to talk to the administrator. The secretary responds by saying, "She's in the building but she's not available just at this moment. If you will let me know how we can be of assistance, perhaps I could have someone else help you, or she could return your call." Once the secretary finds out the purpose of the call, if it turns out to be urgent or an emergency, she will say, "Hold a moment, I can reach her for you." If it turns out to be something that someone else can handle, she puts him in contact with the proper person. If it is a low priority but the caller insists on speaking to the administrator, the secretary can reduce the length of the interruption by saying, "Just a minute, I will interrupt her for you."

6. *Secretary to secretary.*

Most calls should go secretary to secretary. Where there is a need to convey information to another office, the secretary can call the secretary at the other office and leave the message or get the information. Generally, one call does it all when it goes secretary to secretary. If the secretary asks for the administrator, often he will be out; the secretary leaves a message for a return call and this leads to a game of telephone tag.

7. *Angry callers.*

The well-trained secretary can play a valuable team role by taking the anger out of callers before having them speak to anyone else. Secretaries are generally unaware that the administrator wants this done, and so they turn the angry caller over to the administrator as quickly as possible. Such action only exacerbates the situation. The specific steps for handling an angry caller have been explained in Chapter 7.

8. *Shorten calls.*

Informal research reveals that at least half the time spent on the telephone is wasted because the call is longer than necessary. With careful attention the amount of time spent on the telephone can be reduced by fifty percent with no loss of efficiency and with improved public relations. To illustrate how calls are unnecessarily extended, the two most discussed items on the telephone are health and the weather!

The reason health and the weather are discussed is to overcome start-up problems and to create mood. It does not seem comfortable to just pick up the telephone and start talking business, so it is only after talking about extraneous topics that business begins to be discussed.

How can this time-wasting discussion of health and the weather be avoided? Voice tone and inflection can be used to create mood and overcome start-up problems. When the phone is answered the caller says, "Hello, Mary. Will you give me some information about _____?" Mary hears the smile in the voice, so the proper mood has been created. She also is aware of the sense of urgency so she answers promptly. When she has given the information, the caller says, "Thanks, Mary, that's exactly what I needed. You always help me."

This constitutes a very pleasant phone call that avoids time wasting behavior. When the savings are computed at the end of the day, it is found several minutes have been saved on every phone call for the caller and an equal amount for those called. The ability to get down to business with a smile in the voice has paid off to the tune of half an hour that day.

9. *Misdirected calls.*

Calls that reach the switchboard and then go to an incorrect office cause an interruption for the occupant of that office as well as an irritation for the caller. In spite of this, it is normally the practice to put the newest employee on the switchboard. It is acceptable to have a new employee operate the switchboard if he has been well trained. This training needs to be so effective that the operator can receive a vague request for information and get it to the right office the first time. Care should be given to selecting a real professional for this job rather than treating it as a casual assignment.

10. *Group calls.*

Every time a telephone call is about to be made, the question should be asked, "Is this call urgent or an emergency?" If the answer is no, instead of making the call, a note should be made and, after a list of calls is accumulated, all calls on the list are made at one time in a telephoning period that has been set aside in the daily schedule. Making a number of calls in a set period keeps the calls short and avoids interrupting the daily schedule unnecessarily. It is amazing how quickly a large number of calls can be made when they are grouped together on a list.

With proper training the secretary can also group **incoming** calls. When someone calls the office, the secretary blocks the call politely and determines its priority. If it is not urgent, she will then say to the caller something like this: "Will you be in your office between 4:00 and 4:30? You will? All right, we will return your call during that period." In these few seconds the secretary has determined whether or not the person will be available, so that a call will not be made for naught. The secretary has also issued a commitment to the caller that there will be a return call at a specific time. In addition, the procedure prevents an interruption to scheduled activities. This is truly professional behavior on the part of the secretary.

11. *Give authority to secretaries.*

As explained in Chapter 7, the secretary should be instructed to handle telephone calls from beginning to end without involving the administrator. Most secretaries have not been told to do this, so they believe they are supposed to get the name of the caller and pass it on or to take a message when the administrator is not available. When secretaries are given authority and asked to handle calls completely if possible, they will routinely determine the reason someone is calling. Many times they will have the requested information and simply give it to the caller, and most callers will be pleased to get the information without waiting and not be offended because they did not get to talk to the boss.

12. *Redirect calls.*

Many calls come to one office when they really should have gone to another. When the secretary determines this is true, he simply tells the caller that the information needed is available in another office. The secretary then says something like, "The information you need is in another office. I'll connect you." After this, the secretary is careful to take care of good public relations by adding a statement like, "If you don't get the information you need, please call me right back."

13. *Forward calls.*

Any time a call is forwarded to another office, the caller should be given the name of the office to which she is being forwarded and the number of that office. In this way, if the person is cut off they will not have to call back. Additionally, when a caller has to be placed on hold, an update should be given every thirty seconds.

14. *Explain the absence of the administrator.*

Another irritation can be avoided if the caller is always given a plausible and accurate justification for the absence of the administrator. If the administrator is attending a meeting, the secretary would say something like, "Mrs. Jones is not available now. She's attending a staff meeting." The caller is much less likely to be angry if he knows that Mrs. Jones is involved in a meeting rather than absent for no stated reason. If the secretary responds to a caller by saying, "She's out," there is a likelihood that the caller will assume this is untrue. "She is in conference with a teacher," is much more believable because it is specific and has no connotation of evasion.

15. *Conference calls.*

Having conference calls instead of meetings can save a great deal of time and money. Conference calling saves travel time and also ensures that the meeting itself will be more brief because there is less chance of incurring some of the time traps associated with face-to-face meetings. A conference call can be held among workers within a building, a town, or a state rather than having them travel to a meeting at a central place.

16. *Concluding rambling calls.*

No matter how well organized a person may be there is still the problem of other people who call and who are not organized. Another person's poor information or habits must not be allowed to prevail and waste time for both parties to the conversation.

When someone calls and begins to repeat unnecessarily or ramble from the point of the conversation, the other person must become wholesomely assertive and take charge of the call. Being "wholesomely assertive" means this: the person is given a reason why the call must be concluded. The call is brought to a close with a statement like, "I've got to go now; I have to get to a meeting in ten minutes." Or, "I'll have to leave you now; I have a report that has to be finished by ten o'clock." This informs the other person that there is a compelling reason why the conversation must end. Offering a plausible reason will normally prevent any public relations problems.

17. *Organize before calling.*

Prior to picking up the telephone, it is important to have all necessary materials in hand and a plan in mind for conducting the call. It is helpful to consider what the goal is for the call and the sequence of topics which are to be discussed. It may even be necessary to write these down so there is no risk of forgetting the points to be covered.

The same thing would be true when making a personal call. If the family is calling grandmother long distance, it is best to get all family members together and briefly review what each is going to discuss with her. This will make the call more productive, keep it shorter, and ensure that all family members don't ask the same question, e.g., "How are you feeling, grandmother?"

In summary, a little planning and thought about the use of the telephone can pay great dividends in time and money saved. The training of all employees will multiply the savings many times over. The rules for using the telephone are simple and effective when they are consistently applied. When a call is made to an office, the goal is to complete the matter with one call only. For example, a call is placed and the person called is away; the caller then tells the secretary the purpose of the call. The secretary may have the information or she may say, "I'll get the answer and call you back." The caller replies, "You need not reach me, just leave the information with my secretary." The caller was able to conclude the matter, even though the administrator was out and the secretary did not have the answer.

CHAPTER TEN
Manage Stress

Time management and stress management are inextricably linked because people with too much stress naturally waste time as a result of heightened error and accident rates. A wholesome level of stress is necessary in order to be effective but, when the level gets too high, the resulting negative impact reduces effectiveness in work and threatens personal health. Energy is spent in a way that is not productive and is even counterproductive in terms of goals to be achieved. The information in this chapter is designed to help school leaders maintain a healthy level of stress and thus be more effective and happy.

A group of principals were discussing their inservice needs to determine which seminars and programs should be secured for their staffs in the coming year. In the course of this discussion a menu of programs was made available to them, including motivation, time management, effective communication, stress management and leadership skills.

They had done needs assessment surveys with their faculties and were anxious to find programs that spoke to those needs. They were pleased as they perused the list of available subjects and compared them with the needs assessments. But when they got to the stress management seminar they passed it without stopping. They did not want a stress seminar. One principal observed, "It would be nice to have a stress seminar for my employees because they are under a lot of tension, but, since the benefits would be for the employees' personal use, it would be unwise to spend tax dollars on a such a program."

After some consideration they looked again at the needs assessments. They found concerns about such things as absenteeism, student achievement, interpersonal conflicts, accidents, errors, and ways of enhancing student achievement. These topics were of extreme interest to a majority of staff members. They concluded that the stress seminar was probably more important than any other, because unhealthy stress has a tremendous impact on the entire organization and exacerbates the problems listed. Students, teachers and administrators do not perform as well as they are capable when experiencing negative stress.

This is not to say that educators have been totally oblivious to this problem in the past. Teachers, in particular, have been quite sensitive to stress in students. For example, elementary teachers, after recess period, have traditionally had the students put their heads down and rest for a few minutes while listening to soft music.

A secondary teacher whose students were about to take a big examination used a specific technique to reduce stress before the test. The tension was so great that it could be seen on the faces of the students as they entered the room. To reduce this the teacher told them to take out a sheet of paper and put their books away. She gave them ten minutes to write down anything they wanted from memory from their studying and let them keep that paper with them while they took the test. The relief they exhibited was obvious as their demeanor changed from frowns to smiles.

SCHOOL ADMINISTRATION IS HIGH STRESS

Attempts have been made over the years to compare various jobs in terms of the amounts of stress each generates. The results indicate that school administrators are near the top of the scale and in the same high category with physicians, waiters, and business executives. They occupy a position just below the top category, which includes air traffic controllers, police officers and firefighters.

It is obvious that school leaders experience high stress because the fate of employees and students is in their hands and they make many decisions everyday crucial to peoples' lives. They have to evaluate the performance of people, decide who is to be promoted and, in some cases, who must be terminated. No matter how confident they are about the actions they take, they are torn between feelings of compassion and the demands of duty, which often conflict.

In the early 1990s the statistics on death in the United States revealed that fifty-one percent of all deaths other than accidents were due to stress. This is more than the next three leading killers combined: cancer, rheumatoid arthritis, and nervous and mental disorders were responsible for a combined total of just twenty-nine percent of all deaths. There are no stress-related mortality statistics for school administrators as an isolated group, but it is reasonable to believe that the percentage of deaths in this group would be higher than the national average. Additionally, stress is responsible for illnesses that do not immediately cause death but which reduce effectiveness or lead to medical retirements.

AN INCREASING PROBLEM

As civilization progressed, the causes of stress changed from famine, pestilence, exposure to the elements and war to the negative elements of the late twentieth century lifestyle. In the last fifty years there has been an upsurge in stress as Americans moved from a largely agrarian, uncrowded environment to the fast-paced society of today. Major contemporary causes of stress include:

• A Machine-Controlled Environment

In the modern world machines and media devices are allowed to dictate human behavior. The alarm clock rings and people rise whether they are rested or not. They stop or go when the traffic light changes, and telephones are permitted to interrupt the daily schedule. Television packages entertainment into strict thirty-minute segments. Unless vigilance is exercised, machines can dictate a lifestyle, as they can operate constantly without rest; human beings cannot!

• Compacted Living Conditions

The population has steadily moved from a predominantly rural setting to crowded urban living with its high-rise buildings and traffic jams. Packed beaches and long waiting lines at theme parks inject tension even into attempts at recreation, and farms and small towns with their pastoral settings have given way to paths of concrete and tract homes. Friendly smiles are supplanted by expressions of fear or indifference. The small school where the principal knew every student has been replaced by larger, often overcrowded schools with heterogeneous populations. Relatively minor concerns about school discipline have been replaced by the danger of guns and drugs on campus.

• Career Frustration

Budget reductions and the economics of the market place are causing schools and businesses alike to reduce staff. Thousands are losing their jobs altogether, while others who had expected to move forward in their careers find promotions are not available. Schools are being asked to serve a growing population with the same budget or with fewer dollars. Job insecurity is widespread, and a teaching diploma is no longer the guarantee of employment it had been for years.

• Depersonalization

A generation ago most people grew up in a two parent home and in a community where they knew their neighbors. Today many people live in apartment houses where they do not even know the people who live next door. Names have been displaced by numbers, which are required by law to be assigned at birth. Some colleges and high schools no longer have students put their names on exam papers in an attempt at fairness through anonymity. Department stores are much more interested in the customer's account number rather than their name. This impersonal atmosphere reduces human contact and conversations, which in themselves are natural reducers of stress.

• Competition

The free enterprise system is undoubtedly the best economic system ever devised. People put forth their best when they are rewarded for their efforts in comparison to other people. This means, however, there is constant competition between people and this struggle for survival and success produces stress.

• Conflict of Interest

Leaders, and school administrators in particular, frequently find themselves as arbiters caught between conflicting interests. For example, the superintendent of schools receives a demand for lower taxes and simultaneously a demand

71

for a new school program. A school principal is required to rule upon a grievance that one staff member has against another. The decisions that these school leaders make are inevitably going to offend someone. Having to render such judgments puts pressure on the one who must decide.

• **Time Pressure**

School administrators are talented people, and people with talent are in demand. In addition to their personal and professional responsibilities, they are asked to serve in many capacities throughout the community. This often leads to over-commitment and inadequate time to meet all obligations. The "Spread-Too-Thin" syndrome is a frequent stressor of school leaders.

STRESS DEFINED

In the discussion thus far, it's been argued that stress is a threat to mental and physical health and a detriment to work performance. To understand why this is true, one must understand exactly what stress is and the extent of its impact. It is also important to be able to predict what extended exposure to harmful stress will do, so specific defensive actions can be taken.

Stress is a psychologically induced action which brings about potent physiological reactions in the body through the "fight or flight" response. The brain senses danger and sets off a chain of physiological reactions designed to help defend against threats.

The fight or flight response is easy to see in animals. A dog and a cat run upon each other in an alley. The cat's hair stands up and the dog's muscles tense as these two decide to fight or run. In the case of a dog and cat, the cat will probably run up a tree, and the dog will give chase, thus using up the physiological preparations both made for fight or flight.

When prehistoric human beings lived in caves and the caveman came upon a bear, his brain immediately prepared him to fight or outrun the bear. Chemical changes occurred in the caveman's body, all of which made him a faster runner and a more effective bear fighter.

It is an oversimplification, but the problem is that the brain, through the fight or flight response, prepares people today to fight or run when neither response is appropriate in this civilized world. It is not possible to physically fight back at the things that cause stress nor can one run away. Thus, over and over again the body is physiologically prepared for a fight that doesn't happen. Such physiological preparations become a threat to health because they no longer serve a useful purpose; they are no longer used up in meaningful activity.

IMPACT OF STRESS

Whenever symptoms of stress such as edginess, anxiety or fear are present, the brain is getting the body ready to fight. This means that physiological changes are occurring including some or all of the following:

1. *Blood-clotting time speeds up.*

The release of hormones initiated by the brain's recognition of a stressor causes material to be released into the bloodstream to plug a leak in the vascular system. If the cause of the stress was an angry bear, it would be well for the blood to clot rapidly but it does little good when the cause of stress is an angry parent.

2. *Fats in the blood elevate.*

Lipids such as cholesterol and triglycerides elevate dramatically under stress. The more often the elevation occurs, the more likely it is that these lipids will over time attach themselves to the lining of the vascular system and cause diminished blood flow or a blockage.

3. *Sugar pours into the bloodstream.*

Sugar used by muscle tissue for speed and energy is released so a person can run faster than normal. This makes sense if one is trying to outrun a predator, but it does little good against modern stressors.

4. *Muscles tense.*

Stressors cause the muscles in the body to shorten or tense. As the muscles shorten they can cause damage because the area of the vascular system is reduced and blood flow is inhibited.

5. *Blood pressure rises.*

When muscles shorten under stress the pressure on the blood vessels increases as the blood is forced through the reduced area.

6. *Heart pumps faster.*

In order to keep blood flowing to the brain and to other parts of the body, the heart has to pump faster to get the blood through in sufficient quantity to meet the body's needs, even as the capillaries, veins and arteries are reduced in size by pressure from the tensing muscles.

7. *Adrenalin pours in.*

It is known that the presence of adrenalin gives a dramatic increase in strength for a temporary period. Little is known beyond that, but it is generally believed excess adrenalin over a prolonged period can cause damage to vital organs such as the pancreas, liver and kidneys.

RESULTS OF EXTENDED EXPOSURE TO STRESS

Long-term exposure to stress has been documented to be physically harmful. It can lead to the following negative health effects:

• Chronic hypertension

It is normal for the blood pressure to go up when we encounter a stressor. It is also normal for the blood pressure to go down when the event is over. Some people, usually after repeated exposure to stress over a period of years, find that the pressure goes up and stays there. This condition persists even when these individuals are asleep.

Chronic high blood pressure is known as the silent killer. It is estimated as much as one fifth of the population of the United States could have this disease and not know it, because high blood pressure has no symptoms.

• Damaged heart and blood vessels

The physiological impact of stress over an extended period can result in a stroke, aneurysm or damage to the heart muscle itself. Some of these may be mild at first and go unnoticed and a physician may require a treadmill stress test to identify any such damage that has occurred.

• Fatty deposits

The increased lipids in the bloodstream caused by stress can result in fats becoming attached to the lining of the vascular system. A variety of negative results can come from this, such as arteriosclerosis or blood clots.

• Drug reliance

Some people turn to drugs or alcohol to relieve stress. Either can only give temporary relief because the body builds up tolerance and the dosage must be increased as time goes on. Reliance on drugs can lead to addiction and the cure becomes worse than the disease.

MANAGING STRESS — AN ACTION PLAN

Because of differences in personalities and lifestyles, different people must manage their stress in different ways, but there are some general recommendations which should assist all people. These recommendations come from conversations with thousands of school administrators and are designed for the unique needs of this group.

1. *Practice detachment.*

Much of the pressure which school officials feel in their work is not directed at the person but at the position held. Anyone who is doing a conscientious job in one of these positions will incur the wrath of those who want preferred treatment. The school administrator plays a temporary role in any position and must remember that the pressure is directed toward the position rather than the individual.

2. *View from a long-term perspective.*

When something causes worry or an anxious feeling, the question should be asked whether or not this will be of concern ten years hence. In most cases whatever is causing concern now will be forgotten in ten years. Recognizing that most stressors are transitory helps to overcome the feeling that a particular current event is of extreme importance and thus restores the comfort provided by long-term perspective.

3. *Practice defensive time management.*

Buffers should be built into the daily schedule to prevent stress from time pressure. For example, if it takes half an hour to travel to a meeting, the person leaves forty-five minutes early. This fifteen-minute buffer will permit the person to be relaxed while traveling because there is time to spare in case there is an emergency or other delay. Defensive time management also means, in addition to a relaxing personal schedule, shared pressure through delegation, meetings which are enjoyable, reduction of interruptions and a plan for rest and recreation.

4. *Adopt a stress-resistant lifestyle.*

Careful attention must be given to adequate sleep, a leisurely start to the day and built-in periods for rest and relaxation. Emphasis must be given to a life-style which causes one to act contemplatively and listen to what others have to say without cutting them off in mid-sentence. If things start to get hectic or out of control, a person should stop, re-evaluate and make changes until control is regained.

5. *Review personal relationships.*

A great deal of stress results if there are problems with family members or colleagues. It is imperative that everything possible be done to have positive relationships and to avoid conflicts and misunderstandings. Comfort is critical in these key areas. This may require a remedy as simple as becoming a better listener, or it might be as extreme as changing jobs or life-partners.

6. *Follow a proper diet.*

What is eaten can help cause or prevent stress because of the immediate impact food has on the chemistry of the body. A proper diet is one that is low in calories and high in fiber and nutrition, one which consists of fruits and vegetables, whole grains, and protein from sources that do not contain a lot of fat.

It is best to have three light meals a day and it is especially important to eat breakfast. Snacks should not be substituted for meals and careful attention should be given to the amount of salt and sugar consumed.

7. *Exercise regularly.*

It is not necessary to be a marathon runner or even a jogger to get enough exercise to fulfill the requirements of a stress control program. The key to success is regularity; exercise must be done at least three times a week and it must be intense enough to get the heart pumping, blood rushing, and the lungs breathing deeply. Even walking for forty-five minutes at a striding pace will provide enough exercise to meet the requirements of this program.

A strong caution must be given at this point. Every person should have a thorough physical examination and get the approval of a physician before beginning an exercise program. It is also important to have a warm-up period every time exercise is begun.

8. *Pursue leisure activities.*

Benefits are gained when avocational pursuits become a regular part of the schedule. The type of leisure is unimportant as long as the activity is enjoyable and done on a regular basis. Some people choose passive activities, such as stamp collecting, while others like to build things or participate in sports where they combine recreation and exercise. These leisure pursuits should be scheduled just as are all other activities that contribute to good health.

9. *Avoid crutches.*

When stress builds, some people turn to drugs for quick, temporary relief, while others smoke cigarettes or drink caffeine and some overeat. These crutches do no good but can result in a great deal of harm particularly over a period of time as they lead to alcoholism, obesity and pulmonary disease.

10. *Use simple therapies to relieve stress.*

No matter how hard one tries to avoid stress, there will be times when stress occurs and relief is needed. This is when something must be done to bring on the relaxation response, the opposite of the fight or flight response. Fortunately, there are simple therapies which are effective for relieving stress and they do not require a lot of equipment or a great deal of time. At the end of the day, when a person is feeling tired or tense, soaking in a tub of hot water for twenty minutes brings relaxation. Or one can dip washcloths in hot water and rub them on the neck and face, take a brief nap before dinner, sit and listen to music for half an hour or take a stroll. Activities like these and many others have potential for bringing on relaxation and can be easily used.

11. *Work with reason.*

Work is important but it is certainly not the only thing in the world.

The work of a school administrator is really never "done," and many administrators become workaholics because of this fact. Workaholism can only be overcome if a schedule is maintained which includes all of the elements of a successful life. This schedule must include family activities, recreation and exercise in high priority so that work does not crowd them out.

PEOPLE DON'T DIE FROM OVERWORK AS MUCH AS GETTING UPSET ABOUT WORK.

THEY BECOME FRUSTRATED WHEN THEY DON'T FEEL IN CONTROL, AND THIS BRINGS ON KILLER STRESS.

---

12. *Check health regularly.*

Signs of stress can be detected through a thorough physical exam if the physician is asked to look for signs of stress. For example, a test for elevated triglycerides may not be done unless symptoms of stress are being considered. Physical problems which are found can be dealt with best, the earlier they are identified. If there are no findings, anxiety is alleviated and uncertainty relieved, two of the main causes of stress.

13. *Seek professional help if stress continues.*

Most people can bring their stress under control by making simple life changes. In rare cases stress will remain high even though a conscientious effort has been made to deal with the problem. In these few cases individuals need to seek professional help from medical workers and psychologists who are skilled in dealing with the problem.

14. *Smell the flowers.*

These final two steps summarize the previous ones. If busy people like school administrators really took time to smell the flowers, many of the other problems would disappear. This means savoring nature, eating slowly concentrating on the taste of food, and sipping the wine (not more than two ounces in any one day). The pace of life must be leisurely and each day enjoyed because happiness is not a destination; it is a journey.

15. *Help somebody.*

Karl Menninger was once asked, "If a person felt a nervous breakdown coming on what could be done to prevent it?" This great psychiatrist answered without a moment's hesitation. He said, "If somebody felt a breakdown coming on, he should go out and find someone who has a terrible problem which they can't solve by themselves. As he helps someone else, his own problems will be greatly diminished and the breakdown will likely be prevented."

CHAPTER ELEVEN

Communicate Effectively

One of the greatest challenges faced by school administrators is the need to achieve effective two-way communication with a multitude of entities and to do so in an economy of time. They have to discriminate among the materials to be read because so much is written and it varies tremendously in importance from vital to worthless. Priorities must be set in terms of how time is spent providing information to others in the organization and to various publics.

Techniques used for sending and receiving information must be efficient in terms of the goals of the organization. This demands understanding of traditional communication methodology, revelations from contemporary research, current technology and predicted developments in the future. In this chapter recommendations will be made for meeting the dual challenges of dealing with information overload on the one hand, while communicating effectively with everyone involved in the enterprise.

School administrators must be well informed so others can be kept informed. Information has to be acquired and used to persuade students, staff and citizens to support the programs of the schools. Technology and skillful communication techniques will not eliminate the need to make judgments concerning the relative importance of information, but these can help with the mechanics. For example, it was suggested in an earlier chapter that reading be delegated to subordinates, who can process the mass of information in their individual areas of specialty and distil it for the leader's consumption.

A subscription to a computer information service, to newsletters and audio-taped programs will summarize what is happening in education on a weekly or monthly basis. These and similar techniques and devices streamline the processing of information for the busy executive, but sensitivity must be maintained to the inherent dangers of lack of objectivity and completeness of coverage.

In the past decade administrators had to be particularly attentive to court decisions, changes in federal financing of education and innovative programs that garnered national attention. These initiatives had to be interpreted to staff members and explained to the public. Teachers came forward seeking empowerment, and administrators had to learn how to collaborate with them in a mutually acceptable way. Many school boards became interested in strategic planning and directed administrators to install these programs, often to the chagrin of employees who resented this "top-down" approach.

Outcome-based education, which had gotten a strong foothold in the 1990s, suddenly became the target of conservative national groups. Superintendents and principals had to know the program in detail, the motivation of the critics, and how to avoid terms and techniques which would incite both the program backers and the critics. Communication was often clouded by emotion between factions—with school leaders trapped in the middle.

Even the most conscientious efforts still left school leaders at peril as they attempted to stay abreast of everything going on in education. The United States Department of Education presented its Goals 2000 about the same time that major funding cuts were being made in many programs which supported these goals. Most citizens believed these new initiatives from the federal government would be accompanied by financial support, when just the opposite was true. This lack of funding was not explained by officials at the national level; educators were given the unpleasant task of telling the truth to the public.

Not only the federal government put administrators in the position of having to explain innovations and program changes which were in conflict. Every state (and many local school districts) rushed forward with "inclusion," which meant that most special education students would no longer be taught in separate classes but would be returned to the regular classroom instead. The idea was to have teacher specialists work with the regular classroom teacher and the students in what would be a more normal environment. Unfortunately, in many instances when the special education students were placed into the regular classroom, reduction was then made in the state allocation for special education staff. Courageous administrators, who understood that inclusion was being used as an excuse for budget cuts, had to explain this to angry teacher groups, the parents and the public.

The proposals for change will be different in the future. Nonetheless, they will require school administrators to keep abreast of all new proposals. These will then have to be evaluated and explained to all who are involved in every phase of education. Internal communication will have to be effective, and a positive public relations program will need to be maintained. On the one hand, care must be exercised not to over-communicate so that people no longer read or listen nor under-communicate, which could cause alienation as some feel left out of the loop. The following guidelines will help us maintain a program of totally effective communication.

1. *Establish an atmosphere of trust.*

Leaders must be totally honest at all times and candid without being brutal or blunt. As one school administrator described it, everything must be kept on the table so that it is obvious there are no hidden agendas. The goal is to establish an environment where everyone can be heard, where all can disagree without being disagreeable and where all ideas and suggestions are valued. Such an atmosphere requires nurturing on the part the school administrator. The principal who asks for constructive criticism must not become angry when it is given, and suggestions from all staff members must be treated with respect. Steadiness and predictability of disposition are also important; it is detrimental if people have to wait to see what the leader's mood is today before they attempt conversation.

> # LISTENING IS THE MOST POWERFUL COMMUNICATION SKILL FOR LEADERS. WHEN SOMEONE HAS A PROBLEM, THEY DON'T NEED A SOLUTION; THEY NEED A COMPASSIONATE LISTENER WHO WILL HELP THEM BECOME PROBLEM SOLVERS.

2. *Involvement is essential.*

The more staff members are involved in the decision-making process, the more they will understand and be committed to the decisions which are made. The most successful administrators go out of their way to make sure that every staff member is involved as much as possible in the total operation of the organization. This takes time and is not as efficient as having decisions made by one person. But the commitment which results from involvement is worth the extra effort.

3. *Give feedback.*

One of the biggest complaints from teachers and others at the grassroots level is that when requests are made, such as at budget time, they are never told what happened to their requests. A department chair in a high school said that she turned in a request for a certain amount of funds based on what she thought would be needed by her teachers. The amount actually allocated was far less than she requested, and she didn't know where the cuts had been made, by whom or on what basis. She said that next year she would not put much thought into the request.

An elementary principal described a technique he used to avoid this kind of problem and at the same time include involvement and a feeling of "teamness." When he put together the requests from his various departments, he would make a decision as to what would be reasonable to request as an entire school. If his decision meant that the requests from the teachers would have to be reduced (which seems to be the case in most budgeting processes), he would go back to the departments and explain why he had made the reduction. Then he would go a step further, which made the whole process much more palatable. He told the departments how much would have to be cut and then let the individuals involved decide where the cuts would be made. His staff members felt like real partners in this relationship and thus supported the decisions, which were jointly made.

4. Start with a problem rather than a solution.

When decisions are "handed **down**" they are usually resented even if they are excellent. Such autocratic leadership should be replaced by democratic procedures that insure the ideas of all the people in the organization can be tapped. This approach reflects the idea that the best answers do not reside in one or two individuals but in that reservoir of people who make up the entire organization.

A superintendent said her cabinet members were complaining of being overworked, while at the same time she had some additional tasks that had to be undertaken. If she had asked for volunteers for the new tasks, she was certain there would be none. So she employed a technique which moved these busy, overworked people to volunteer for extra duty.

At a meeting of her cabinet, she laid out the new challenges and, instead of proposing possible solutions, she asked her cabinet members if they had any ideas how these new jobs might be tackled. She correctly anticipated what would happen when these problems were placed before creative people who were used to solving problems. Immediately, they started to make suggestions and before very long, they had developed a plan for getting the extra jobs done and eagerly volunteered to perform the work. The superintendent summarized by telling why her technique worked. "When people give birth to a proposal, they will do whatever is necessary to make sure that it succeeds. I challenged them with a problem; they developed solutions that were their own."

5. Generate enthusiasm.

The tone of a school or school district emanates from leadership and thus enthusiasm must be generated in a variety of ways. The convocation of teachers at the beginning of the school year is an example of how enthusiasm can be shared. It is customary in most districts for the superintendent, board president, and the head of the teacher association to bring greetings. These are usually brief and upbeat and set a positive tone for the year.

If the superintendent acknowledges there are any problems, this is followed by a positive statement to the effect that "Together we can handle the tasks we face; we are going to have a great year." Problems become challenges because of the leader's enthusiastic approach, and this enthusiasm is contagious and the staff becomes motivated.

The superintendent could exacerbate any problems by injecting negative thoughts into the tone of the greeting. In one instance the superintendent reviewed what staff members later called his "litany of doom." There was no smile on his face as he talked about the immense problems they would all be facing. He talked about the increase in the premiums for health insurance, the lack of a pay raise, the maintenance that did not get done over the summer and the supplies that would arrive late in the school year. By the time he finished talking, the teachers were depressed and slumped in their chairs; this was not what these teachers needed to help them face a new school year.

6. *Be a good listener.*

Listening is a powerful communication skill, which must be cultivated and emphasized particularly by veteran administrators. It is likely that the administrator has heard many times the problem someone is going to present. However, it must be kept in mind what this person needs most is a compassionate listener rather than an answer or a solution from the leader. If they are cut off rather than given a hearing, they are denied the very thing they need: someone in authority to listen to their concerns. Leaders must guard against making assumptions after hearing only a small part of what someone is saying, because the assumptions are often incorrect.

The benefits that can be achieved by active listening are many. Four are listed here as illustrative examples:

A. *Lowering tension* — when persons are upset, their stress can be reduced, and they can be returned to stability by another's listening to them.

B. *Building self-image* — when interest is shown in someone through listening to what they have to say, their ego needs will be met. The undivided attention demonstrates that the leader feels the person is important.

C. *Problem solving* — Problems can be solved and people can be educated to be problem solvers if leaders will ask three questions: What is the problem? What can you do about it? What will be the consequence of your action? Not only will this help a person solve an immediate problem but it is an approach which can be used as new problems arise in the future.

D. *Reducing anger* — Conflict between individuals often leads to lingering anger, but this situation can be remedied through listening. One individual initiates the conversation by asking a question and then listens. The conversation would probably go like this,

"I don't feel that we are getting along as well we should. How do you feel?" Then the initiator listens without making retorts while the other person goes through the phases of catharsis, sympathy, and self-evaluation. If the one who initiates the conversation has done an honest job of self-evaluation, when the third phase is reached by the other party, there will likely be a meeting of the minds and an elimination of tension with its time-wasting results.

7. *Write to explain, not to entertain.*

In written communication the goal is to be clear, brief and positive, avoiding flowery phrases and complicated sentence construction. Preference should be given to simple sentences, short paragraphs and one-page letters whenever possible. Readers deserve written communication that is well organized and looks good from a mechanical standpoint. Correct spelling and punctuation are absolute musts, and copy editing and proofreading should be done by someone other than the author. It is particularly important to have written material scrutinized by several people, if it is to be distributed widely.

8. *Productive confronting.*

School administrators often have to communicate with people in situations where there is a strong difference of viewpoint. These confrontations can deteriorate so that nothing positive is achieved or the situation is made worse. Such negative outcomes can often be reduced if leaders seek, and have a plan for, "win-win" negotiations. The aim is to find an accommodation so that both parties feel successful rather than having one be a winner and the other a loser.

To prepare for productive confronting, it should be determined in advance what the parameters are for compromise, what can be sacrificed without violating convictions or giving up more than can be afforded. The amount of power which can be exercised should be gauged realizing that the amount will be different when dealing with subordinates compared to dealing with a superior. The negotiations should be pleasant, straightforward, free of anger, and the goal of mutual satisfaction should be constantly emphasized.

9. *Public speaking.*

School leaders are called upon to make many oral presentations to all sorts of groups. Rarely are two presentations on the same topic as is the case with professional public speakers who give the same speech over and over. School administrators known for giving effective speeches generally follow these guidelines:

• *Get down to business quickly.* Very little time is spent at the beginning of the speech discussing extraneous matters. If humor is used it is tasteful and of very short duration. Within a couple of minutes at the beginning the speaker is into the body of the presentation.

• *Tell them what you plan to tell them (introduction.)* The speaker prepares the audience by briefly letting them know the purpose of the presentation. "Today I am going to tell you why you should vote for my candidate."

• *Tell them (the body of the speech.)* This is the major part of the speech where the speaker goes point by point presenting the information (without rambling off the subject). "Here are five major reasons why she deserves your vote."

• *Tell them what you told them (summary.)* The speaker summarizes by repeating the main idea of the speech. "For these reasons I urge you to vote for her."

• *Brevity is the key.* Excellent organization is essential for giving a short speech, and *everybody enjoys a short speech*. It is incumbent on the speaker to be well organized so that information can be presented in a brief time span.

Supreme Court Justice and author Oliver Wendell Holmes was asked to give a speech. He inquired, "How long do you want me to speak?" When asked what difference that would make, Justice Holmes replied, "If I can speak for an hour, I'm ready right now. If you want me to speak half an hour, I'll need several days to prepare. If you want me to speak twenty minutes, I will need at least a week to get organized."

It is advisable to have an outline of the points to be covered in the speech. This will reduce nervousness and insure that everything is covered. Under no circumstances should a speech be read; the audience will be lost in a very few minutes.

10. *Covert communication.*

School administrators communicate constantly through their behavior. For example, the amount of trust in subordinates is shown by the amount of freedom they are given; less supervision shows trust, while too much supervision communicates distrust. The posture of an individual tells people whether or not that person is pleased with what is going on, and gestures convey whether or not that person is pleased. Even apparently harmless phrases can have covert meanings different from what the words say technically. For example, a person prepares to leave home in the morning and the spouse says, "Are you going to wear that hat?" This is not a question but rather a negative comment about the hat.

Care should be given to making covert messages harmonize with each other (gestures match words, etc.) and with the intended meaning. Poor communication is at the top of the list of things that waste time when people work together; the challenge for everyone and especially for leaders is to send clear, positive and consistent messages through all the mediums used.

The following true story demonstrates how administrators must always be vigilant. (The names of the characters in this vignette have been changed for obvious reasons.) A high-school principal had three assistants, one of whom had been with him only a couple of months. The principal noticed the staff members did not seem to accord the new assistant principal the respect they gave the other two.

"I was at a loss to know why he was given so little respect," the principal said. One day he was sitting in his office talking with a faculty member who was also a close friend. He asked his colleague if he had any idea why the teachers ignored this new assistant principal. His friend looked at him and asked if he really wanted to know the answer to that question. He assured him that he did; he was surprised by his reply.

"The faculty doesn't respect him because you don't respect him," his friend said. "When Silas gets up and speaks, you sit with an approving smile on your face. When Lenore makes a presentation, you do the same. But when Samuel makes an announcement or gives instructions, as soon he sits down, you immediately get up and repeat what he said. It's obvious you don't have confidence in him, so how can we?" When he thought about it, he knew his colleague was right. He was the culprit; he was sending the message of lack of confidence and doing so covertly.

11. *Use technology.*

Rapid change is occurring and will continue to occur in the world of communications as computers propel educators down the information highway. It is important that these advances are evaluated and exploited to the maximum to sharpen communications and save time. Care must also be taken to guard against misuse, which wastes time and harms public relations.

For example, voice mail can make people feel that everything is being done to serve them efficiently or it can make them feel abused by the number of redirections. The fax machine can be a lifesaver in certain situations or it can be the recipient of unwanted advertisements. Whether these devices are positive or negative depends to a great degree on how they are controlled.

To keep abreast of what technology is currently available requires the services of a specialist to give advice. Salespeople have too strong a vested interest to provide the kind of help needed, and the field is too specialized for school administrators to hope to study enough to stay on the cutting edge. An objective expert can give the guidance needed in a relatively short amount of time and at a reasonable cost.

12. *Information agencies.*

A subscription to an information service will be an increasingly beneficial investment as the volume of information grows. Whether the information is received via computer or audio cassette, some accountability system is needed to see that personnel actually use what is purchased. Leaders will also need to schedule purchase of these materials before they become stale.

Listening to a summary of events in education on audio cassette while driving seems a wise use of leadership time. The cassettes can be shared by several administrators, thus reducing the cost per person.

13. *Communication audits.*

It is generally known that universities and private companies provide audits for educational institutions in a variety of areas. Financial and organization structure audits are best known, but communication audits are available too, most often done as a part of a broader study. A communications audit can be done separately at little expense. Sampling is done of information flow among staff, students and the community. Recommendations based on the findings are made for inservice programs, publications and other tactics to enhance overall communications.

CHAPTER TWELVE
Motivate Staff

Time and effort devoted to motivating staff members bring quick rewards because of increased effort on the part of these workers. One can imagine what it would be like if every student, every teacher and every other employee came to their assignments each day "fired up" with enthusiasm, the ultimate goal of motivation. Conversely, it is shocking to contemplate how much time and money are wasted by people who are not properly motivated. This is why leaders must give constant attention to this extremely important phase of leadership. The payoffs and the penalties are great.

A consultant had been working over a period of years with the administrators in a large urban school district in California. There was a change of superintendents and, for a period of three years, she did not visit the district. When she returned to do a workshop after this hiatus, she found the administrators very excited about what had happened at one of the high schools during this period. It is an excellent example of a real turnaround school and what causes such dramatic change.

The school was formerly a terrible place for staff and students alike; someone called it the Devil's Island of education. The building was dirty, the walls were covered with graffiti, and student attendance was the worst in the district. One got the feeling that everyone in the school had capitulated. Teachers who wanted to do a good job were often assigned to that school as a testing ground and then moved to another school when they had paid their dues. Several principals had attempted to make improvements but with little success; the problems overwhelmed their attempts to resolve them, and they left, or stayed and succumbed to the malaise.

The consultant was skeptical when she was told the situation had changed and now the school was a showplace where students and teachers took pride in their work. The attendance percentage had risen into the high nineties, the graffiti was gone, the depressing atmosphere had been replaced by the excitement which comes from a sense of growth and achievement. The dramatic changes being described were so immense, the consultant was anxious to see for herself.

A day or so later she had an afternoon free and called the school to get permission to visit. The principal seemed very pleased when he gave her his hearty approval. She arrived at the school and visited the principal's office, so that someone would be aware she was in the building. Instead of letting her tour on her own, the principal said he would be pleased to show her around personally.

"Before we start our tour," he said, "I want you to meet somebody who's very special." He introduced the consultant to his secretary and proceeded to say some very complimentary things about her. "I don't know what I'd do without her; she's my right arm. She's determined to make this the best school in the district." His secretary beamed with pleasure.

They started down the hallway and he stopped and introduced her to his head custodian. "Look at the pride this man and his staff take in this building. You have been a high-school principal; you know how great it is to have someone keep the building in tip-top shape." The head custodian was all smiles as he shook the visitor's hand.

A few more steps down the hall and he introduced her to an English teacher and told her what a great job she was doing with some students who had special needs. They met the cafeteria manager and he told her how great the food was and how this manager only hired people who loved youngsters. And so it went around the entire building; every person they met received specific compliments for something they were doing.

When they got back to his office, the consultant said, "I could see what you were doing out there. You probably did more to motivate your staff in one hour than some principals will do in a whole year. Do you ever get accused of being a glad-hander?"

"I wasn't glad-handing," he said, "Everything I said about those people was absolutely true."

"Don't they have weaknesses?" she asked. "Don't they have improvements that are needed and that you are working on with them?"

"Of course they do," he replied, "They are human beings. But people don't grow when you call attention to their weaknesses; they grow when you call attention to their strengths."

Of course he was right. He was doing what all leaders should do to get their employees working with greatest enthusiasm. He was calling attention to their strengths and praising their achievements. This is why leaders who make comments only when there is something to criticize will not have subordinates who get joy from their job or who work with the utmost zeal. Every study of effective schools reveals the most important ingredient in making a school great is the principal. A common characteristic of principals of effective schools is they take specific actions on a regular basis to stimulate employees, and they do not overlook opportunities to motivate. As one superintendent observed, "You've got to have a principal who is a cheerleader or the school will never be the best it can be."

When people work together in harmony, the power of the team is greater than the sum of the team members. Additionally, if staff members are not on the team, they may even use their energies to work against the goals of the organization. Those who feel alienated at first ignore the activities of the group, and if the alienation continues, they may actually attack and become roadblocks to progress. The team approach is essential to get these individuals to embrace the goals rather than ignore or attack. When "teamness" is achieved, the power of the corporate endeavor can reach its peak as positive energies flow from all staff members.

Since it is apparent that the best chance for improving production and performance is to motivate the staff and since it is also true that unmotivated employees will be the biggest time wasters, the question becomes, "What will really work in getting people to give peak performance?" Researchers reveal that people do not give maximum effort to any cause until they feel a need to do so. When something occurs to satisfy these felt needs, they are motivated to give their best efforts to the cause. The challenge for leadership is to discover the needs people are feeling (or to create needs within them) and supply a satisfier for those needs.

When dealing with school teachers and other employees in the educational enterprise, it is possible to eliminate consideration of the most basic needs people feel. If the challenge was to motivate individuals who are living in poverty, satisfiers such as money, improved working conditions and job security could be used because those to be motivated would likely be feeling the need for survival, comfort and regular employment. Those to be motivated in the educational setting will, in all probability, have already had these needs met. A higher level of needs and satisfiers must be considered by school administrators.

The following chart identifies the needs often articulated by professional people; beside each need is a possible satisfier which might be employed.

	NEED	SATISFIER
1.	Use all talents.	Assignments which use them.

A principal discovered that one of his teachers was an excellent fiddle player specializing in bluegrass music. He called upon her to perform frequently at faculty parties, assemblies, etc. He said her commitment to the entire organization was improved when he tapped her talents. "Since then I try to discover and tap all of the special talents of my teachers because it makes for a stronger team," he said.

	NEED	SATISFIER
2.	Have work recognized.	Praise.

One school district uses a page in the newsletter to list those staff members who are doing special projects or trying new ideas. Local newspapers can be used to recognize special achievements of staff and students. The Superintendent of the

Laredo School District in Texas recognizes staff members who achieve perfect attendance by giving a sizeable cash award at a public ceremony—tangible praise indeed!

3.	NEED	SATISFIER
	Belong to a team	Involve people

An elementary principal has each staff member preside at faculty meetings on a rotating basis. She says this is one of many signals that all staff members are on one team.

4.	NEED	SATISFIER
	Experience growth	Measurable goals

The evaluation instrument used in one school has a section entitled, "Goals for Growth." These are determined jointly by the administrators and subordinates and reviewed periodically. The job targets help document growth much as wise teachers remind students of what they have learned.

5.	NEED	SATISFIER
	Gain responsibility	Enlarge the job

When tasks are done well, greater freedom and authority are extended. With each success more power is assigned to this successful individual so that the job grows as rapidly as the person.

6.	NEED	SATISFIER
	Achieve advancement	Promote when earned

Even-handed advancement of people based solely on merit is essential. One superintendent said, "Everybody knows who is going to get the job because they know I will give it to the best prepared, hardest working and most deserving person rather than making a decision based on any other considerations. If I were to deviate from this policy, my employees would not work as hard because they could not be assured that hard work would lead to advancement."

Once the premise is accepted that every member of the organization is probably underutilized and is capable of making greater contributions if motivated, certain guidelines can help meet this challenge of reaching everyone.

A: All people basically want to succeed.

A principal told the story of how she put this axiom to the test. She had been in a workshop where the statement was made that all people want to succeed. She couldn't bring herself to believe this because of the trouble she was having with one of her staff members whom she referred to as her "lounge lizard." She had written him off as a hopeless case because of his negative attitude toward everything that went on in the school. He was inconsistent with his students, sarcastic, lethargic and unkempt in his personal appearance. It was said that he had been a great teacher earlier in his career.

She decided to make one last attempt to see if there was any need in him to succeed and feel accepted. She put him in charge of a project that would keep him in the public eye and, because it was his alone to do rather than assigned to a committee, it would be obvious when the job was done whether or not he had succeeded. She announced his assignment in a faculty meeting and expressed confidence he would do a good job.

To her amazement and that of the faculty, he took hold of the job (after some halting steps at the beginning) and brought it to closure with great success. Additionally, his disposition and appearance improved and he did a better job in the classroom. She concluded her story by saying that at least part of the problem was with her. "The need which he was expressing through his behavior should have been a signal for me to act. Once he was given a chance to get recognition through positive acts, his needs were satisfied and he no longer felt compelled to get attention in negative ways. I believe it is true that all people want to succeed if we can find the right approach."

B: People work harder after each success.

There is a trap which leaders can fall into if they are not careful, and that is the human tendency to call attention to things which are wrong rather than to things which are right. Every achievement must be recognized and failures not accentuated. It is imperative that junior administrators be taught this axiom early in their careers, because it is contrary to instinctive feelings. Programs designed to guarantee that the good work of all subordinates is recognized must be fundamental. Positive reinforcement must be constantly emphasized so that it becomes a habit for all school leaders.

C: People are goal-seeking.

At the very least, all who work in an enterprise must know the goals which have been chosen for the organization. In terms of motivation, a far better way is to develop organizational goals cooperatively involving every person in the process. Ownership brings with it commitment.

A principal called a meeting of his custodial staff and sat in as his head custodian conducted the session. She had asked them to discuss and make suggestions about how the rigorous summer cleaning could be done and still permit summer vacations. A lively discussion ensued and a plan was hammered out. All went away happily committed to the schedule which they had developed.

D: People enjoy work.

Leaders sometimes feel that their subordinates would avoid work if they had the choice. What is known from psychology does not support that stance but rather indicates people enjoy work if they get satisfaction from what they are doing and if they get recognition from their superiors. The challenge is to cause people to want to work hard by recognizing their achievements and by never overlooking the effort which someone gives.

E: Give subordinates as much freedom as possible.

The administrators of a school district were discussing time clocks, which had just been put in their schools. Apparently it was felt that a few teachers had been coming in late or leaving early, so time clocks were installed without consulting any of the teachers as a simple way to control the offenders. The vast majority of teachers reacted emotionally to what they saw as unprofessional treatment. Additional hours teachers had been giving to their jobs without extra compensation were greatly curtailed. The extra control and, in turn, the loss of freedom these professionals felt, reduced their level of enthusiasm. The school district, and more importantly the students, were losers because of this ill-conceived action.

The obligation of leaders to motivate staff is a crucial one. A systematic program directed toward motivation must be put in place and constantly monitored. Motivated people work hard and save time; people who are not reached will perform at less than their potential.

CHAPTER THIRTEEN
Identify Time Wasters

In this chapter a summary of the main time wasters will be presented. Many have been cited earlier in this book, and all are based on what school administrators have perceived as impediments to efficient use of time. Such identifications have emerged from discussion groups of educators. For example, an administrators' inservice meeting made up of a variety of school leaders, including superintendents, principals, assistant principals and central office personnel identified eleven "universal" time wasters: generic categories which can be divided into narrower, more specific time wasters. These were listed in two groups under the headings of internal and external.

INTERNAL TIME WASTERS
LACK OF DELEGATION
FIRE FIGHTING
LACK OF PLANS
LACK OF PRIORITIES
OPEN DOOR POLICY
PROCRASTINATION

EXTERNAL TIME WASTERS
TELEPHONE
MEETINGS
VISITORS
PAPERWORK
DELAYS

After these broad groupings of universal time wasters were considered, a small group activity was initiated to determine how they might appear as specific behaviors in the everyday lives of individuals.

For example, a broad category like "lack of planning" might be an umbrella over a number of smaller, more specific time wasters all with that generic theme. The groups were then given the task of breaking the large categories down into specific events, which they recognized as having an impact on their own professional lives.

In seven minutes, the groups had identified twenty-three of what were called personal time wasters. Some items had a tendency to overlap but were included to insure there would be no gaps. The following is a listing of the items identified by this diverse group (and it is typical of those produced by similar groups). Possible solutions which they subsequently developed are also included.

1. *Lack of planning.*

The participants observed that even though they knew the value of planning, little was actually done on a daily, weekly or longer-term basis. Low priority tasks and minor crises rushed in to fill the void left by an absence of priorities. A great deal of energy was expended during the day, but because of a lack of focus little accomplishment could be shown for the energy expended.

The groups agreed that they would have to take stronger control of their lives so that they would not be solely at the mercy of others. Only a true emergency should be permitted to interfere with the daily schedule. If these emergencies occur frequently, time should be built into the schedule to handle such emergencies.

If the time is provided, but emergencies do not occur on a given day, a standby task should be available to fill that void. The conclusion reached was that any day that is planned will be more productive than a day not planned, even if unanticipated interruptions occur.

TIME WASTERS ARE ESSENTIALLY THE SAME FOR ALL BUSY PEOPLE. FORTUNATELY, ONCE IDENTIFIED THEY CAN BE ELIMINATED WITH MINIMAL EFFORT.

---

2. *Underchallenged subordinates.*

The workshop participants talked about how some teachers and other staff members are not well motivated. What is more, some school leaders accept the status quo without making an effort to remedy the situation, which leads to some employees being overworked while others do not do their share. This imbalance of productivity lowers morale.

Several solutions were proposed for improving this situation including the even-handed assignment of work to all employees. It was also suggested that the school leaders should focus upon those who are not making a full contribution and that specific techniques should be developed for getting them motivated. Suggestions included giving special assignments, developing individual contracts, counseling and setting short-term goals so that praise could be given frequently. Staff members who are not contributing fully should continue to be a challenge to leadership until ways are found to require every member of the team to reach peak performance.

3. *Lack of training.*

The discussion about lack of training centered around the fact that it is often assumed a person can perform a certain skill just because they have a certificate issued by some agency. The consensus seemed to be that it is necessary to check the skills of every employee to see if they are capable of performing at the level which is desired. Employees must be hired who have the skills necessary, or a program must be devised to provide those skills in on-the-job training. Workshops to provide specific skills and mentoring programs to give generalized training were also proposed to fulfill this need.

4. *Crisis syndrome.*

It was agreed that a crisis atmosphere leads to a high error rate and a generally unpleasant feeling among staff members. The predominant atmosphere of the work place should be one of calm, with crises occuring rarely.

A technique for achieving this involved holding a meeting on a regular basis with the principal, superintendent or other leader and the subordinate staff. At this meeting the leader asks three questions: What crises have been experienced in the last three months? What could have been done to prevent these? What crises can reasonably be expected in the next three months?

A brief discussion of these three points prepares the staff to tackle events in the future. Dealing with crises in retrospect reassures people by having them identify actions which could have been taken and which might have prevented the crisis.

There are very few crises that cannot be anticipated if people are thinking ahead. Additionally, having one person designated as the one who will act in case something unanticipated occurs has a calming effect on the personnel involved.

5. *Haphazard exposure.*

A principal said that he tried to go to the bathroom as infrequently as possible because anytime he left his office, he could expect to hold several informal conferences in the hallway before he returned. Another person reported that drop-in visitors took up a great deal of her day.

It is generally agreed by those who have dealt with the problem that much can be done to reduce unplanned contacts. One suggestion was to have a predictable time each day to be available. One principal said he tried to meet his staff members at the door each morning, while another said he tried to be in the lounge one hour each day so that by the end of the week he had been available to every teacher. The idea for the leader is to be available on a planned basis known to all staff members.

6. *Being over-specialized*

The challenge for leaders is to know what is going on in the organization by judging the outcomes from each department rather than to dig deep into a subordinate's area of responsibility. If the chief executive officer knows as much about what an employee is doing as the immediate supervisor, then supervision is being duplicated, causing confusion and wasted time.

A superintendent put it this way, "If I know everything that's going on in my transportation department such as the minute details of finances and the performance of each person who drives a bus, then why do I need a transportation supervisor? What I need to know is that the employees are happy and the buses run safely within the budget which is appropriated. These outcomes which provide the big picture give me all I need to know."

7. *Being under-specialized.*

A reading specialist said that she spent at least twenty percent of her time typing, so one fifth of her day was not with teachers and students. When school administrators find themselves doing clerical work, it is obvious that a professional resource is being improperly spent.

A solution would be to support professionals with persons who can perform clerical skills more efficiently and at a lower cost, and in that way the professional and the paraprofessional would both be effectively utilized.

One principal told of a network of senior volunteers who had been recruited to serve his school when the budget did not provide for paid employees. He said they trained and monitored their own members, worked on a regular basis with little absenteeism and never caused any difficulty. This way he kept his staff members from being under-specialized by doing tasks which did not require professional training.

8. *Unnecessary or poorly held meetings.*

Every year or so there is a national study done to determine how much time is wasted in various types of activities. The results are always about the same; at least eighty percent of the time spent in meetings is identified as wasted time. This represents a great monetary loss as was pointed out in an earlier chapter, but the negative impact on morale is probably more profound. Prior to the holding of each meeting a test must be applied to see whether or not the meeting is necessary or whether it is going to be held just because it was scheduled.

It is also important that meetings not start "from scratch." An example would be a meeting where no preliminary work has been done, no agenda developed and the participants just thrash around until a direction is chosen. It is much better for a leader to present a goal or objective at the beginning of the session plus at least a skeleton of how the goal might be pursued. There might be several possible directions or tentative approaches presented to the participants with the understanding that these are examples only and not an exhaustive list.

The challenge is for the leader (or possibly a subcommittee of the large group) to provide enough direction to get the group moving without providing so much information that little is left for the group participants to contribute. There is a delicate line between the proper preparation to get a meeting moving and going too far, so that group members feel they are simply ratifying what has already been decided.

9. *Indecision.*

Leadership philosophy can have a profound impact upon the proper utilization of time. Laissez-faire leadership (actually an absence of leadership) causes indecision to prevail throughout the organization. Individuals and small groups go off on their own, and there is little coordination among departments.

Autocratic leadership is undesirable because one person dominates the organization, and this lends to a lack of motivation on the part of the staff members. Instead of time being lost through indecision, it is dissipated through lack of enthusiasm and resentment of domination.

Democratic leadership should be employed so individuals can be motivated through involvement. Admittedly, this form of leadership moves more slowly but, by using the proper mechanisms, democratic leadership can be employed in an economy of time. The prevailing opinion that democratic techniques have to be unwieldy and complicated is not invariably true.

10. *Lack of deadlines.*

Setting deadlines is a simple technique but a real timesaving idea if used properly. Deadlines which are mutually adopted and understood by all should be assigned to every job. Tasks without deadlines tend to expand unnecessarily, becoming the victims of procrastination and getting lost in the scale of priorities. When an assignment is given to another person it is important that a discussion be held concerning a reasonable deadline for its completion.

Deadlines should be used when the assignment is given to oneself. For example, when making the "To Do" list each day, instead of writing 10:00 to 10:45 work on the proposal, it is restated and a deadline is set by writing, from 10:00 to 10:45 *complete* the proposal.

11. *Failure to use travel time.*

A superintendent reported that he did a study to determine how much of his week was spent traveling between schools and to meetings where he represented his school district. His study revealed and other studies seem to agree with his assessment, that nearly one full day each week is consumed in travel.

He said he made profitable use of his time by doing such things as using his cellular phone to return calls which had to be made by him personally. He also used the time for dictating letters and reminders to himself. His testimony was that this large chunk of time which previously was wasted is now used in a very productive way.

12. *Poorly arranged space.*

School buildings and central office complexes often grow "like Topsy" with insufficient thought and planning of how the arrangement of space will service or hinder productivity. Lack of planning in this area can cause a continued loss of time because of the built-in inefficiencies in the system.

Within individual offices a study should be done to determine how space is utilized relative to the availability of machines and materials regularly employed. Changes can be made which implement a better working flow in most cases.

Within a school district remodeling of its administration building, a new floorplan illustrates how the functioning of an organization can be enhanced by proper use of space. In the old configuration, the superintendent's office was just off the entrance lobby and thus quite vulnerable to drop-in visitors and other types of interruptions. Some of the high-traffic offices were located in the rear of the building and drew a lot of traffic past all the other offices. When the renovation was done, the superintendent's office was moved to the rear of the building, and personnel, payroll and procurement were moved to the front and near the lobby because of the high traffic these functions generate.

13. *Insufficient delegation of authority.*

Poor delegation was dealt with at length in a previous chapter so little more needs to be said here. One group of administrators probably summed it up best when they said, "It is a waste of time to check on people if they are doing good work on a consistent basis." They also agreed that decisions should be made at each level in the hierarchy of administration and only unusual items should move to the next higher level.

14. *Overlapping assignments.*

Job descriptions must be constructed in such a way that all staff members know which tasks are theirs and which are the responsibility of another person. When assignments overlap, time is wasted in a variety of ways including the interpersonal conflicts that arise when more than one person has responsibility for a given task.

A variation of this time waster can happen even to an individual. A middle school principal said that she had been making multiple trips to the same place each month and realized that with better planning she could make one trip instead of several and avoid the duplication.

15. *Poor sense of humor.*

A frown, negative comment, use of sarcasm or other such acts on the part of the leader will chill the enthusiasm of subordinates and inject time-wasting tension into the organization. Leaders must, particularly at the beginning of the day, smile and be pleasant when dealing with staff at all levels. A smile and a consistently pleasant disposition are musts for the leader who wishes to inspire workers and prevent their being tentative.

16. *Disappearing without notice.*

Good cooperation between colleagues and subordinates creates a synergy that enhances productivity and provides a good working atmosphere. One thing that works contrarily to this goal (particularly for secretaries) is for the administrator to fail to communicate effectively. An example is leaving the office without notifying others of the destination and return time. Stating your intended whereabouts before leaving is a habit which must be cultivated in the interests of saving time and promoting harmony among colleagues.

17. *Playing favorites.*

A very real time waster in many schools is the uneven assignment of work. Teachers have traditionally expected to teach brighter students and have fewer classes as they gained seniority. Those who get favored treatment want to exploit the situation further and those who are given a disproportionately heavy load resent it; both groups are dissatisfied.

Even-handed assignment of tasks without playing favorites is essential to the morale of everyone. It was agreed that there was no better image than that acquired by a fair leader who expects the best performance possible from everyone and who gives no one an unfair load for any reason, including seniority.

18. *Poor use of technology.*

Introduction of new technology can be difficult because of the fear that accompanies change, a fear affecting most of the people in the organization. This fear can be overcome if individuals have an opportunity to learn the new technologies without pressure and to understand the benefits that will accrue to them personally.

Changes should be implemented gradually so that employees can be made to feel secure. This means that pacing is important, neither going too fast, which would alarm the employees, nor going too slow so that interest is not maintained. The leader of the organization must be the one to set the tone and lead in establishing a pace that will result in wholesome change.

19. *Messiness.*

Tidiness not only provides a more pleasing environment but it also saves time. Messy desks, bulging filing cabinets cause confusion, and computer discs which contain outdated information lead to a high error rate.

Good trash basket skills on the part of the leader are important mainly for the example set for others. A messy office signals a leader who is not in control, while a tidy well-organized office reassures people who observe the obviously organized work area.

20. *Blaming others.*

When a mistake is made, there is a natural tendency to try to find a scapegoat so that the blame can be placed elsewhere. This wastes time and creates insecurity among colleagues who feel they may be unjustly accused. The way to save time and provide security for all involved is to adhere to the principle which says, "When a mistake is made it should be admitted, corrected and work should continue with a minimum of interruption."

21. *Lack of signage.*

Routine information which is needed on a recurring basis should be placed on a sign to reduce interruptions. A good locator board in the lobby will direct visitors to the various offices. If a special meeting is to be held in the building on a given day a sign can be placed in the lobby directing the participants to the correct room. In addition to saving time public relations will be enhanced when helpful, positive signs are used which make visitors feel welcome.

22. Inattention to needs of co-workers.

One individual who is experiencing difficulty can cause a problem for the whole organization. The major theme should be, "A chain is only as strong as its weakest link." When a member of the organization is going through a period of emotional challenge, others should be willing to pick up some of the slack so that the entire organization does not suffer. The goal is to be helpful and sensitive to the needs of co-workers without being nosy. When a team member has a problem, others come forward quietly and tactfully to provide assistance without embarrassing the one who is temporarily impaired.

23. Fatigue.

People who work when they are tired will experience a disproportionately high error rate, which probably means that the work is not being done well. A better way is to recognize fatigue and rest and rejuvenate before continuing work.

A principal told of how he stayed up late one night doing paperwork at his home; the next day his productivity was low, his temper was short and he got much less done than he normally would have. If he had rested the night before he would have come to his job with renewed energy and a positive disposition. Rest is not just a luxury; it is essential for maintaining high-quality performance.

CHAPTER FOURTEEN

Train the Staff

When school executives experience a good time management inservice training they naturally get excited about the possible changes that can be made to improve their work habits and their personal lives. There is a great deal of motivation that results as leaders work together in a group activity and develop their own simple but effective changes, which can be implemented immediately with modest effort. The difficulty is to get this enthusiasm to transfer to other members of the staff when the participant returns to work. The people back home have not been fired up by the seminar experience, and so resistance is shown and progress is minimized. A good way to overcome this phenomenon is to provide an opportunity on site for other staff members to participate in a structured activity. This is superior to asking workers to read a book. However, many are inspired to read a book as follow-up to a group activity.

It became apparent that some vehicle was needed to assist the seminar attendees to spread the timesaving information through the entire organization. As one principal stated it, "I go to a workshop or read a book and get excited. But I have difficulty structuring a training program for others. It takes too much time, so I just don't do it. Most books need one more chapter which contains a study guide for teaching the information."

It was obvious that, if a training program were prepared and put into the hands of those doing the training, the resulting consistency and completeness would enhance the effectiveness of the instruction. Thus, a chapter has been provided in this book to assist those who want to provide "in house" time management training.

Techniques will be given first for an informal workshop designed for a brief time period. Then materials and instructions will be given for a more extensive training program which will provide information and activities for in-depth training. The study guide for the extended workshop also serves as a summary of the entire book.

A "MINI" TIME MANAGEMENT INSERVICE

These brief activities can be done in less than an hour and are quite effective for a small group such as the personnel of a department or the faculty of a small school. The leader needs no particular expertise in time management.

Step One:
Organize participants into brainstorming groups of three persons. Achieve as much diversity as possible by not letting people who work in the same office (teach the same grade, do the same task) be in the same group. Select a chairperson for the group by using some non-threatening technique, such as counting off or birthday earliest in the year, etc.

Step Two:
Have the leader of each small group conduct a brainstorming session of ten minutes identifying as many time wasters as possible. The workshop leader should get the groups started by suggesting a couple such as poor communication, extended coffee breaks, etc. Then the small groups add to the list other time wasters which they have experienced or observed at work.

Step Three:
Have the chairpersons of the groups take turns in reading their lists aloud. Participants will probably be surprised to see how similar the various lists will be.

Step Four:
Compliment the groups for their productivity in such a short time and explain to them that they have just done the first step in problem-solving. Step one in problem-solving is to identify and define the problem.

Step Five:
Give participants another ten minutes to work in small groups and have them come up with the solutions to as many of the problems as they can in the time allotted.

Step Six:
Have the groups share their solutions. Remind them that they identified their problems and came up with their own solutions rather than receiving them from an outside expert.

It is quite likely that those who developed the solutions will carry them out because people follow through on their own ideas. Where this mini-seminar has been attempted, positive results accrued to the group. Some experience more improvement than others, but all report gains from the exercise.

A TIME MANAGEMENT TRAINING PROGRAM

The following outline can be used for a full-day program or excerpts may be selected for a shorter period of training. The leader lectures or leads a discussion based upon the text which is provided. Transparencies are projected on a screen using an overhead projector or the outlines contained in the text can be placed on a flip chart. In either case, these will need to be done in advance of the seminar.

The quiz which appears in Chapter 2 of this book will also have to be reproduced in advance or a copy of this book can be given to each participant. The lecture/discussion then moves forward as outlined in the pages to follow. Please note: the leader must have read the entire text of this book. To assist the leader each topic has a reference to the chapter where material on the subject is contained.

Copyright law prohibits the reproduction of material in this book. However, the quiz in Chapter 2 and material in Chapter 14 entitled "Train The Staff" may be reproduced and used for training of its own employees by any school, school district or entity which operates on a nonprofit basis. No charge may be made for participation in any such training exercise or mini-seminar beyond the cost of materials. Credit must be given to Dr. Ivan W. Fitzwater as the author and to Pro>Active Publications, 10 Hale St., Rockport, Massachusetts 01966 as the publisher. For permission to use the seminar materials in other contexts, contact Pro>Active Publications.

APPENDIX

TRANSPARENCY ONE
(Refer to Chapters One and Two)

This introduction is designed to generate anticipation, to outline the purposes of the seminar and let the participants know what type of activities will be included. They will be led to reflect upon what is now happening in their lives and to think about how the situation might be changed and improved.

Participants will recognize that they are now having problems managing time but they will be encouraged by the possible benefits to come when they hear how others have been helped. Time for success and happiness will be the goal as the current stereotype of the harassed executive is challenged.

Transparency One gives an overview of the entire workshop. Each item on the list should be discussed briefly by the seminar leader.

PURPOSES OF THE WORKSHOP

1. **BUILDING A SENSITIVITY TO TIME AS AN IMPORTANT RESOURCE**
   A. Uniqueness of the time resource
   B. Value to be gained by using time savers
   C. Exploding the workaholic myth
   D. Positive experiences of others

2. **REVIEWING OUR CURRENT USE OF TIME**
   A. The diagnostic quiz
   B. Identifying our time wasters

3. **FINDING WAYS TO IMPROVE THE USE OF TIME**
   A. Planning and goal setting
   B. Building delegation skills
   C. Blocking interruptions
   D. Effective meetings
   E. Identifying time savers

4. **IMPROVING COMMUNICATION**
   A. With superiors, subordinates, and peers
   B. Achieving a more pleasant work atmosphere

5. **REDUCE STRESS AND THE CRISIS ATMOSPHERE**
   A. Time management is self management
   B. Impact of stress on individuals
   C. What stress does to learning
   D. Work fewer hours by working smarter

EXERCISE NUMBER ONE
Diagnostic Quiz

Each participant is to take the diagnostic quiz which is in Chapter Two of this book. If the participants have copies of the book they can simply answer on a separate sheet or, if the quiz has been reproduced beforehand, they can answer on their individual copies.

They should be told that some of the questions may not make sense as they are answering them but there is a purpose for each which will be revealed later. When they have completed the quiz they should add up the number which they have marked "Yes" and the number which they have marked "No."

INDIVIDUAL ACTIVITY

Time should be given so that all of the participants have completed the quiz. Then they should be told that the proper answer to every question on the quiz would be "No." For every "Yes" there will be information given so that growth and improvement can occur in that area.

The leader can use the information in Chapter Two of this book to tell why the answer to every question should be "No." If participants have their own copies of the book a brief discussion can be held for each question. These discussions will have to be brief; two to three minutes on each question is the maximum available if all other topics are to be covered adequately.

TRANSPARENCY TWO

Some participants (perhaps many) will come to the inservice feeling their situations are unique and thus, their problems have no solutions. Some feel their difficulties are all attributable to other people and thus beyond their own control. As gently as possible (and in a non-threatening way which would turn off many people), the workshop must get the participants to realize that there is something which *they* can do.

They can improve their situation if they correctly identify the causes of the problems and then take action. This becomes apparent as they see the causes of problems are not always other people or situations beyond their control. This transparency is designed to show that we may be our own worst enemies and we can change and improve.

WHO IS TO BLAME?

PROBLEM	CAUSE
UNPLANNED INTERRUPTIONS	FAILURE TO DELEGATE AND IMPROPER OPEN DOOR POLICY
LACK OF SOLUTIONS	FAILURE TO TRAIN BY EMPLOYERS
UNCLEAR GOALS IN ORGANIZATION	FAILURE TO PLAN COOPERATIVELY
EMPLOYEE MISTAKES	FAILURE TO PROVIDE TRAINING & WHOLESOME ACCOUNTABILITY
EMPLOYEE PERSONAL PROBLEMS COMING TO YOU	FAILURE TO HAVE LEADERS AT LOWER LEVELS PARTICIPATE
TOO MUCH MAIL	POOR UTILIZATION OF SECRETARY
LOW MORALE	INSENSITIVE LEADERS POOR MEETINGS

WE MAY BE THE CULPRITS!

TRANSPARENCY THREE
GETTING ORGANIZED
(Refer To Chapter Three)

The time spent planning is quickly paid back through a reduction in the amount to time it takes to do a task. One minute in planning saves twenty minutes in doing; this has been demonstrated in numerous research projects. It is imperative to get the participants to understand that planning doesn't take time; it saves time because of the reduction in execution time.

Each of the points on the transparency should be reviewed through lecture and discussion. Participants who have not been planning may become a little bit defensive at this point. Rather than confront them it would be well to listen to their points of view and just say, "You may be right, let's see how we feel after we've looked at a number of the other topics."

ORGANIZE YOUR DAY

A. Make a list of everything that must be done today.

B. Which items on the list *must* be done by me?

C. What items can be delegated?

D. Choose the most important item on the list and start on that item.

E. Make sure unpleasant jobs are done early in the day.

F. Do one thing at a time from beginning to end.

SMALL GROUP ACTIVITY TIME WASTERS EXERCISE

After the participants are organized into small groups of three to five, a leader is appointed to guide the group through the time waster exercise. The challenge given to the groups is to brainstorm and identify as many time wasters as they can in ten minutes. Anything which wastes time anywhere can be included on the list, not just time wasters which occur at work.

The leader should give a couple of examples which the students can put at the top of their list to get them started. The workshop leader should move among the groups during the activity so that if any group gets "stuck" a suggestion can be made.

TRANSPARENCY FOUR
DELEGATION
(Refer to Chapter Five)

The leader should discuss the fact that lack of delegation is one of the biggest time wasters in educational leadership. A review of the benefits of good delegation and the common roadblocks to delegation would be helpful at this point. It would also be a good time to debunk the prevailing stereotype which says that each time a person gets promoted, she will have to work longer hours. Good delegation can prevent this.

If a group activity is needed after the transparency is covered, participants can return to their small groups for a discussion of effective delegation, and each group member can be asked to identify at least three things which he or she has been doing in the past that should be delegated.

EFFECTIVE DELEGATION

A. Delegate in outcome terms. (Don't tell people how to do things — agree on what is to be achieved and let them figure out how.)

B. Give the whole job to one individual.

C. Use a tickler file to stay on top of deadlines.

D. Eliminate the "I must do it myself" syndrome.

E. Be on guard for reverse delegation.

TRANSPARENCY FIVE
EFFECTIVE MEETINGS
(Refer to Chapter Six)

The reputation of an organization is often determined by the quality of its meetings. Unfortunately, in most situations employees do not feel meeting time is used profitably; they may even dread going to meetings. Time can be saved and morale strengthened when leaders understand the importance of implementing steps to insure quality meetings.

MEETINGS

A. Send agenda in advance.

B. Hold meeting only when involvement is needed. (Never use for announcements.)

C. Start on time.

D. Outline purposes and activities at beginning.

E. Announce ending time. (Never run overtime, because this kills morale.)

F. Include only the appropriate people.

G. Never repeat anything for latecomers.

H. End with the question, "Did we accomplish what we set out to do?"

I. Hold meetings under ideal conditions.

1. Temperature, lighting, etc.

2. Free from distractions and interruptions.

3. Avoid overcrowding.

4. Have an effective leader.

TRANSPARENCY SIX
Proper Use of Secretary
(Refer to Chapter Seven)

The secretary is often the most under-utilized resource in a school or office. Upgrading the participation of this valuable staff member involves a change of perspective on the part of the leader and the secretary.

This important person can do more than routine clerical tasks. The stereotype must be changed so the secretary can perform higher-level tasks than those traditionally given. The secretary becomes an office manager and team-mate of the administrator.

THE SECRETARY

A. Operate the office on a team basis.

B. Build secretarial self-esteem.

C. Let the secretary plan.

D. Assign as an extension of the leader.

E. Use highest-level talents.

F. Handle visitors.

G. Screen calls.

H. Write letters.

I. Manage schedules.

TRANSPARENCY SEVEN
Reducing Interruptions
(Refer to Chapter Eight)

Interruptions break the train of thought and waste time by constantly causing one to start over. They have become such a part of life that they seem legitimate until put into perspective by examination of work patterns.

Careful deliberation upon the points given as ways to deal with interruptions will provide many solutions. Each participant may have a different idea of the meaning of these points, and so an exchange of such ideas is a productive exercise.

If an activity is desired at this point, simply have the participants go back into their small groups and brainstorm for seven minutes listing the most likely interruptions experienced by school administrators.

INTERRUPTIONS

THE MOST COMMON INTERRUPTIONS:

... Drop-In Visitor

... Improper use of In-Basket

... Telephone

... Desk Clutter and General Untidiness

... Crises

HOW TO TAKE CONTROL:

... Set Reception Hours

... Have Secretary Screen Everything

... Set Time Limits on Visits

... Hold Stand-Up Meetings

... Have Regular Rap Sessions with Staff

... Group Telephone Calls

... Shorten All Telephone Calls

... Come to Work Early Rather Than Stay Late

... Go to Subordinate's Office

... Meet Visitors in Lobby

... Be Out

TRANSPARENCY EIGHT
Saving Time on the Telephone
(Refer to Chapter Nine)

Elaboration upon the points on this transparency will pay immediate dividends for the participants. This device, which was invented to save time, can become the worst interrupter. This transparency will guide the participants as they exploit the potential of the telephone while avoiding its pitfalls.

THE TELEPHONE

1. Use to prevent travel.

2. Delegate routine calls.

3. Shorten calls.

4. Reduce misdirected calls.

5. Let secretary give out information.

6. Redirect calls without offending.

7. Forward calls properly.

8. Use conference calls rather than meetings.

9. Deal firmly with disorganized callers.

10. Have calls go from secretary to secretary.

11. Emphasize positive public relations.

12. Use E-mail instead.

TRANSPARENCY NINE
Managing Stress
(Refer to Chapter Ten)

A discussion should be held of the ways stress and time management are inextricably bound together. The presenter should review the impact which stress has upon an individual and upon an organization. Particular attention should be given to the impact of negative stress on learning.

If an activity is desired, the participants should return to their small groups and brainstorm about an ideal day for a school executive. They can make a plan which could be used as a prescription by a practicing administrator. All activities would be listed from the time the person rises until he or she goes to bed that night. Remind the participants that they are being asked to dream a little and picture what would be ideal.

STRESS MANAGEMENT

1. Adopt a proper diet.

2. Have regular exercise.

3. Change your lifestyle.
   a. Decide to take charge.
   b. Review personal relationships.
   c. Build in buffers.
   d. Work with reason.
   e. Check health regularly.
   f. Use simple therapies.
   g. Avoid crutches.
   h. Develop leisure pursuits.
   i. Take time to smell the flowers.

TRANSPARENCY TEN
Closing Summary

The participants should be cautioned about making too many changes in too short a time. The idea is to grow through evolution rather than revolution. An effective technique is to have the participants make a list of five things they are going to do as a result of the inservice. As these are effectively put into use, additional changes can be identified and implemented.

The final activity is to go over ten concepts that summarize in generic terms all of the information which has been included in the workshop.

To Save Time

1. Make a list to organize the day.

2. Do the most important task first.

3. Delegate to all subordinates.

4. Set chunks of time for tough problems.

5. Cut back on meetings.

6. Eliminate needless reports and record keeping.

7. Reduce circulating of materials.

8. Use otherwise idle time.

9. Plan, act, evaluate in a cycle.

10. Use rest, relaxation and recreation as rewards for good work.

Index

absence, explaining, 66
administrators (see under specific
    title, e.g., *assistant principal*)
adrenaline, 74
agenda
    daily, 57
    meeting, 42
alcohol, 74, 77
alienation, 90
analysis-paralysis, 10
architecture, school
    (See *space arrangement*)
assistant principal, 31, 61
assistant superintendent, 37
audio texts, 86
audits
    communication, 86

blocking calls (see *screening*)
blood clotting, 73
blood pressure, 73
budgeting, 81
budget reductions, 71, 80, 81

cafeteria manager, 89
California, 88
cholesterol, 73
communication, 79ff.
    audits, 86
    covert, 85
    written, 84
competition, 71
computers, 86
conflict of interest, 71
confrontation, 84
convention meetings, 43
correspondence, 16, 84
copyright, 105
covert communication, 85
crisis management, 4

criticism, 80
custodian, 89, 93
Cycle of Planning, 19

deadlines, 13, 14, 98
    anticipating, 14
    tracking, 13
decision making, 10, 81
defensive time management, 75
delegation, 30ff., 99
    reverse, 35
desk
    organization of, 14
detachment, 75
Devil's Island, 88
drugs, 74

E-mail, 125
effective schools, 89
eighty-twenty principle, 20
elementary school, 60
elementary teachers, 32
emergencies, 8, 12
employee motivation, 12, 89ff., 96
empowerment
    of teachers, 79
evaluation conference, 26
exercise, 76

faculty meetings, 11
fatty deposits, 73-74
fight or flight, 72, 77
football coach, 20

glad handing, 89
goals, 23ff.
Goals 2000, 80
goal setting, 23, 26ff.
    exercise, 28
Goals for Growth, 91

graduation, 20
group training, 105

health, 16
Holmes, Oliver W., 85
hypertension, 74
humor, 11, 100

in-basket, 15, 55
inclusion, 80
indecision, 98
in-house time management course,
    103ff.
inservice training, 10, 30, 103
interruptions, 8, 11, 53ff.
information, 79ff.
    flow, 87
information agencies, 86

latecomers, 41
lateness, 12, 38
letter writing, 16
leisure, 76

listening, 83ff.
    active, 83

mail,8, 51
    junk, 6,8
meetings, 11, 38ff., 98
    agenda, 41, 42
    costs of, 40
    room, 41
    stand-up, 57
Menninger, Karl, 78
mini-time-management seminar,
    104ff.
modeling
    of behavior, 22
    of planning, 22

National Academy for
    School Executives, 30
newsletter, 90
nutrition, 76

office door, 11, 53
    policy, 54
office manager, 48
optimism, 22
organization
    daily, 114
outcome-based education, 79

paper, 14, 32, 37
paperwork, 10, 14, 16
    delegation of, 36
perfectionism, 34
personal relationships, 76
physical examination, 16, 24, 78
planning, 18, 19ff.
    cycle of, 19
    lack of, 95
    organizational, 21
police, 61
principal, 18, 26, 31, 53, 55, 89, 92,
    93, 94 (see also *assistant principal*)
problem solving, 10, 82, 83
procrastination, 16
productivity, 19
promotion, 91
public speaking, 84
public relations, school, 46, 80

quiz
    on time management, 6

reading
    delegation of, 31
reception hours, 55
recreation, 76
research, 17
reverse delegation, 35

131

scheduling, 12, 53
  of appointments, 50
screening
  of calls, 64
  of visitors, 51, 56
secretary, 3, 8, 9, 37, 45ff.,
  and calls, 63ff.
  and planning, 51
  criteria for selecting, 46
  interviewing, 49
  office manager, 48
  public relations, 46
signs, 55, 101
  locator, 55
site-based management, 10
space arrangement, 99
speeches (see *public speaking*)
Spread-Too-Thin syndrome
staff
  motivation, 32, 33, 89ff., 96
  training, 32, 103ff.
stress, 69ff.
  defined, 72
  in school administration, 70
students, 31
  discipline, 30-31
superintendent, 22, 24, 35, 37, 54,
  82, 94
switchboard, school, 46, 61, 62
  operator, 62

teachers, 30, 32, 37, 38, 54, 69 ,81,
  93
  motivation of, 22
teaching, 22, 30
teaming, 21, 46, 50, 82, 90
technology, 86
telephone calls, 47, 58
  conference, 66
  delegation of, 9, 51
  forwarding of, 66

handling information requests,
  62ff.
  irate, 47ff., 64
  misdirected, 65
  routine, 9
time clocks, 93

time management, 16
  and self-management, 5
time wasters, 94ff.
training, 96
  staff, 103ff.
travel time, 63, 99

United Way, 25

vacations, 2, 15
  canceling, 15
visitors, 56
voice mail, 62, 86

workaholism, 3